A JEWISH CALENDAR *of* FESTIVE FOODS

by JANE PORTNOY

Calendar Commentary by MARSHALL PORTNOY

Illustrations by ROBIN REIKES

Designed by MEGAN CLARK

Photography by BILL NYBERG

Primary Title Font: Bodoni
Primary Body Font: Avenir

ISBN: 978-1-615-33631-2
Library of Congress Control Number: 2010909151

Printed by Jostens, USA

To Helen and Max · *With Gratitude*

To Marshall · *With Love*

To Julie and Michael · *With Hope*

TABLE *of* CONTENTS

ACKNOWLEDGMENTS

The completion of this work has been a long time coming. This recipe collection spans over half a century, and encompasses so many people and places in my life.

I remember with appreciation Amy Hamburg and Rachel Ginsberg, then teenagers, who helped me convert handwritten recipes into typed form.

Kathleen Wilson is a superb executive assistant at Temple University. She was excited about this project, and she helped me format the document into a computer-friendly form. Thanks also to my friend Irene MacDonald, ever the enthusiastic booster.

Thanks to the wonderful team at Jostens, especially Paula Shelton and Rita Pleimann, for their expertise and support.

I am grateful to my close friends Marjory Bildersee, Susan Callen, Susan Klempner and Elaine Weisberg who continue to be interested in this project, and who have tested and critiqued recipes. They have long endured progress reports about the book. Now that it is completed, they can stop asking, "When already?"

My sincere thanks to Marjory Bildersee, Lynne Breslau, Susan Callen and Rabbi David Straus for taking on the tedious job of proofreading. Any errors that remain are entirely my responsibility.

Bill Nyberg is a superstar in the world of ophthalmic photography. I am so grateful that he took on my project, and he continues to be very helpful and supportive.

I can't say enough about my graphic designer Megan Clark, a true artist who never fails to answer my endless emails with cheerfulness and promptness. She is always responsive and collaborative when I offer my opinion, but I usually defer to her because her judgment is pitch perfect.

It was love at first sight when I saw Robin Reikes' work. Robin translated the joy, humor and tradition of the Jewish holidays into her delightful illustrations. It is no accident that both of us have blond sons named Michael who serve as some of the inspiration for the mischievous little guy in her pictures.

My admiration and appreciation go to my husband Cantor Marshall Portnoy for his eloquent and informative commentary on the Jewish calendar. A life-long love for the subject informs his writing. He makes a sometimes confusing and mysterious topic interesting and approachable.

I am grateful to him and to our children Julie and Michael who spent much time on this project, particularly as willing tasters and reviewers during the testing process! Additionally, I thank Julie for identifying my graphic designer Megan Clark, and Michael for his back cover illustration concept and his beautiful cake decoration on page 117.

Finally, thank you to my parents — to my Dad for instilling a love of Jewish tradition and to my Mom, the best cook around. We spent many, many hours in the kitchen together, and she taught me most of what I know. My love of cooking and baking can be attributed directly to her. Thanks, Mom.

- Jane Portnoy

PREFACE

The book you are holding began simply enough. I wanted my children to have the recipes for the Jewish holiday foods they love. Because the holidays fall very specifically within an elegant framework, I realized that I could not discuss our foods without reference to our calendar. That calendar of course is very different from the Gregorian calendar and, for many American Jews, its structure can be puzzling. Why does Chanukah come at a different time each year? Why do the High Holidays seem to come "early" or "late"? Why is the Jewish New Year celebrated during the seventh month? This cookbook/calendar answers these and other questions, and gives you superb recipes collected over a lifetime of culinary celebration.

I grew up in the rich ethnic atmosphere of Long Island of the 1950's, during a prosperous and relatively peaceful time. Our generation had not suffered the privations of the Depression or the horrors of the Holocaust — the Korean War seemed far away, and the Vietnam conflict had not yet emerged. Woodmere at that time was undeveloped; it was safe and we ran free. We loved to explore the shells of the new homes that were being built by the dozen. When we roamed the construction sites, we picked up metal discs from the ground and pretended they were precious coins. I can still smell the fresh wood, cement and paint.

Populated mainly by middle class Jewish families who had moved out from Brooklyn and the Bronx, Woodmere was close to the beach but still only forty-five minutes from New York City. The new suburbanites brought an incredible ethnic culture to the Island, and it seemed to me that we had the best of everything, particularly in the variety of foods.

Guided by my mother Helen, a patient and excellent teacher, I learned cooking and baking at a young age. Exceptionally gifted, she inherited an incomparable palate which she combined with a native creativity and inventiveness. In addition to solid culinary technique, she knew the little tricks that transform good cooking into artistry. She taught me to put the glass mixing bowl in the freezer before I whipped cream. She demonstrated the secrets of a great vinaigrette dressing. As I grew up, I watched Julia and Martha with enjoyment but, in truth, learned more from Mom.

Max, my father, was a Renaissance man with diverse interests and talents. Raised in a little *shtetl* in the Ukraine, he immigrated to the United States in 1913. Ahead of his time in many ways, he was the only one in our neighborhood with a compost heap! He was concerned about the environment and cautioned me about wasting water. He had an interest in health food and organic gardening. He could draw, and he loved woodworking. He reminisced about the fragrant rolls that his mother baked at four in the morning or about her wonderful blintzes. His views on food preparation were definitely traditional — he did not want to shop or cook! But I can remember two things that he did enjoy making. He tried to recreate the blintzes, and they weren't bad. And he always took on the job of buying and then preparing his incendiary grated horseradish for Passover. We would all groan when we saw the knobby roots appear in the kitchen. We knew that we were in for an unpleasant aroma during the preparation. Oh well, we did have the hottest horseradish on the South Shore of Long Island!

I began collecting recipes from my mother's friends when I was about twelve. At first, I collected only desserts. Then, whenever I encountered a special dish, I asked for the recipe. Recipes therefore became much more than food, but also links to special people, places, and memories. This collection of recipes is my roadmap for holiday meals. The recipes have all been tested and are geared to the home cook. In this volume I present one menu for each chapter with accompanying recipes. I also include additional recipes appropriate for the holiday. As a busy working person, I prefer to buy some items, such as challah or gefilte fish, that are ready-made. These recipes conform to the dietary laws, and a brief summary of these laws is included in the appendix.

- Jane Portnoy

ABOUT THE
JEWISH CALENDAR

L ook at the moon. When you gaze at it, you may believe you are looking at something that is simply beautiful. When you look at it through Jewish eyes, though, you are looking at the heavenly body that provides the structure of the life of our people, the holidays we celebrate, the family times we cherish, the foods we eat.

In ancient days our people looked at the moon as well. They studied it. Without telescopes, without computers, they discerned the phases of the moon and used this knowledge to fashion their months, their years, their lives — in fact, our months, years and lives as well. The month begins when the moon is about to start a new phase. Indeed, the word for month, *"chodesh"*, is the same as the word for new, *"chadash"*. The new moon signals renewal, a fresh start — almost like a miniature Yom Kippur occurring every four weeks or so.

Did you know that you can tell the approximate Hebrew date by looking at the moon? The phases of the moon begin with complete darkness. This is the "new moon", what appears to be no moon (of course, the moon is there, but completely in shadow). This is the beginning of the new Jewish month. Then you will see just a tiny sliver of light on the right side. The month has begun. Every night, the right side of the moon appears bigger and bigger, the crescent enlarging. After about seven days, we see what looks like half a pie in the evening sky.

DAY 1   DAY 7   DAY 14

Full moon means that it's around the fourteenth or fifteenth, and our month is half over. This is doubtless the most memorable part of the month, and it is no accident that many of our holidays came to be at this dramatic time:

> SUKKOT is on the 15th of Tishri.
> TU B'SHEVAT is on the 15th of Shevat.
> PURIM is on the 14th of Adar.
> PASSOVER is on the 15th of Nisan.

Now watch the moon as it grows darker and darker. The last two weeks of the moon's cycle are like a mirror image of the first. After the full moon, light remains only on the left side. Half a "left-illuminated" pie means the month is about three weeks old. That pie will get smaller and smaller until a crescent on the moon's left side means our month is concluded.

DAY 21   DAY 28

Let's say that it takes the moon about twenty-nine and a half days to revolve around the earth — and we call that "a moon" or a month. But we also know that it takes the earth three hundred and sixty-five days to revolve around the sun — and we call that a year. So, if we were to say that twelve "moons" make a year, we would have quite a problem. Twenty-nine and a half days times twelve is three hundred and fifty-four days, not three hundred and sixty-five.

If we were to leave it at that, any point strictly in "moon time" would, every single solar year, occur about eleven days earlier. For example, Chanukah might be on December 15 one year, then December 4 the following year, then November 23 and so on. Pretty soon, we'd be eating potato latkes and celebrating July Fourth on the same day!

In order to add the necessary time to the lunar calendar, we add one month to the calendar seven times in nineteen years. Yes, in seven years out of nineteen, there will be, not twelve, but thirteen months in a year. This is called a leap year. The extra month, which we add in the late winter, obviously has the effect of "pushing" all post-winter holidays later. Rosh Hashanah, therefore, might come just after Labor Day one year, in mid-September another, and sometimes as late as early October. Yet, while there is some variation, it will always come around the time that summer changes to autumn.

The cycle of nineteen years, called a "*machzor*", is special to our people. The word literally means "cycle", and is the same Hebrew word for the High Holiday prayerbook. On September 14, 2015 — Rosh Hashanah 5776 — we will begin our three hundred fourth such cycle, hopefully inscribed in the Book of Life and Blessing.

CHAPTER 1

TISHRI

TISHRI

DATES *of* THE JEWISH HOLIDAYS IN TISHRI

1-2 TISHRI:
ROSH HASHANAH

Rosh Hashanah is traditionally the 1st and 2nd of Tishri; most
Reform Jews observe only the first day.

•

10 TISHRI:
YOM KIPPUR

•

15-22 (23) TISHRI:
SUKKOT AND SIMCHAT TORAH

As will be discussed later in this chapter, there are variations in
practice with respect to the dates on which Jews celebrate this
holiday. Orthodox and Conservative Jews who live outside of
Israel celebrate Sukkot from the 15th through the 22nd of Tishri.
The 22nd day has its own name, Shemini Atzeret (translated as
"The Eighth Day of Assembly"). Such Jews observe the 15th,
16th, 22nd and 23rd as full holidays. The days in between, the
17th through the 21st, are called "Chol Hamo'ed" which means
weekdays within the holiday. The observance of Simchat Torah
is celebrated on the 23rd of Tishri. For traditional Jews the full
observance is nine days.

In Israel, however, only the 15th and 22nd days are considered
full holidays, Shemini Atzeret is combined with Simchat Torah
on the 22nd of Tishri. Thus the full observance in Israel is eight
days. Most Reform Jews worldwide follow Israeli practice.

ROSH HASHANAH

An American calendar begins with January, and one would think that a book about the Jewish calendar would also begin with the first month, which is Nisan, the month in which we celebrate Passover. The Bible refers to Nisan, not Tishri, as "the first month". Yet this book, like most discussions about the calendar (or indeed like any Jewish calendar itself), begins with the seventh month, Tishri. Well, on a humorous note, if our Hebrew alphabet is read backwards, perhaps it's not so surprising that our New Year is celebrated in the middle of the calendar!

So why is the Jewish New Year completely unrelated to the "first month"? Why is Rosh Hashanah celebrated on the first day of the seventh month?

Part of the explanation is found in the Torah itself which makes no reference to this holiday as a "new year". It was simply called the Day of the Sounding of the Shofar (Leviticus 23:24; Numbers 29:1). And, while we often wish one another a *shana tova* which means "a good year", we never call the holiday a *shana chadasha* — a "new year". Even in the Talmud, the Rabbis do not refer to the holiday as the New Year, but as the Head of the Year. It may seem a small point, but the Rabbis were perhaps making a distinction between a legal new year — what we might term a fiscal year or legal year in which budgets, laws and terms of office take effect — and a popular new year, in which we renew ourselves as a people. This is after all not that different from common practice. When somebody says, "See you next year," it's a good bet they don't mean "See you after January 1". They probably mean, "See you after the summer" or "See you in September". That's the time when we return from vacation, from camp or from other summer activities, and take up the normal rhythm of our work, schooling and family life.

It's probably for that reason that the seventh month, and not the first, is the most prominent in Judaism. It's after the summer that we are together once more, and we look forward to making the year ahead a good and blessed one. We promise ourselves to do better in school, make more time for family, or write that novel we'd always had in the back of our minds! The seventh month is the time of personal and collective beginnings. It's a fresh start, a clean slate — it's a New Year.

Of course, the number seven has always had a magical hold on our people. The Sabbath is the seventh day, there are seven weeks between the Exodus and the giving of the Torah, certain animals entered the ark seven by seven, there are seven patriarchs and matriarchs — one could go on and on. So, it's appropriate that the seventh month in the calendar is really the premier month in the hearts of our people. And it is from the first day of the seventh month that our years are numbered.

And what an all-star holiday cast appears on the stage of Tishri! We blow the ram's horn for Rosh Hashanah, we fast on Yom Kippur, we build outdoor dwellings on Sukkot, and we begin once more the yearly cycle of reading the Law on Simchat Torah. Jewishly speaking, that's about "as good as it gets!"

Because of the mathematical relationship between the Jewish calendar and the Gregorian calendar discussed earlier, Rosh Hashanah can fall as early as the first week in September or as late as the first week in October. Therefore the date of Rosh Hashanah will naturally affect the date of the other holidays. For example, there are always about twelve weeks between Rosh Hashanah and Chanukah. So, if Rosh Hashanah falls on October 4, as it did in 2005, then Chanukah will fall very late in December. Chanukah in 2005 did in fact coincide with Christmas, a very rare occurrence indeed!

By the way, for those of you already planning your summer vacation for 2013, you might want to think about returning home early. That will be the earliest that Rosh Hashanah will fall for hundreds of years in relation to the Gregorian calendar, just three days after Labor Day. On the other hand, you can make up for this in 2043 with an extra long summer vacation. Rosh Hashanah will not come until October 5.

Whenever they are celebrated, the High Holidays are a captivating time of new beginnings and hopes, self-evaluation, forgiveness and renewal. Ten days after Rosh Hashanah, we contemplate our actions of the previous year and resolve to do better in the year ahead. We reach out to those we may have wronged in order to renew and heal relationships. And we renew ourselves in services replete with traditional prayers and beloved melodies.

At home, there is tradition as well — in the foods that symbolize the joy of this season. There is honey in the hopes of a sweet year ahead and rounded foods like apples and challah as we pray that our lives may come around to the next Rosh Hashanah in health, blessing and peace.

MENU *for* ROSH HASHANAH

Apples and Honey

•

Chopped Liver

•

Round Challah

•

Gefilte Fish with Horseradish

•

Chicken Soup with Matzah Balls

•

Barbecued Brisket

•

Kasha Varnishkes

•

Green Beans (Page 85)

•

Honey Cake

•

Jewish Apple Cake

•

Chilled Grapes

TISHRI

APPLES & HONEY

3 Granny Smith apples
3 Red Delicious apples
Fresh lemon juice
Honey

Cut unpeeled apples in quarters and remove cores. Slice each quarter in halves or thirds as you desire. Sprinkle with lemon juice to prevent discoloration. Pass apples to guests who can dip slices in individual small bowls of honey. Apples are best if not sliced more than one hour before serving since mild discoloration may occur even with lemon juice.

Yield: 48 slices or more depending on how you slice the apples

After you dip the apple into the honey, but before tasting, say the bracha:

Baruch Ata Adonay, Eloheinu Melech Ha-olam, Borei P'ree Ha'etz,

which means

Blessed Are You, O Lord, Our God, Ruler of the Universe, Who Created the Fruit of Trees.

After eating a bite of the apple, say the following:

Y'hee Ratzon Milfanecha, Adonay Eloheinu Velohey Avoteinu, Shet'chadesh Aleinu Shana Tova Um'tukah,

which means

May it be Your will, our God and God of our ancestors, that You renew the year ahead for us as a good and sweet one.

CHOPPED LIVER

This recipe is best when made the day before so that all ingredients are thoroughly set.

2 medium yellow onions, peeled and sliced
3 tablespoons vegetable oil *or* 2 tablespoons rendered chicken fat and 1 tablespoon oil
1 pound chicken livers, rinsed. *Cut livers in half and trim connective tissue as needed.*
½ teaspoon salt
Pepper to taste
¼ teaspoon dried thyme leaves
1 hard-boiled egg
1 hard-boiled egg yolk for garnish
Crackers or matzah for serving

Sauté onions in oil (or chicken fat and oil) over medium high heat until golden (about 4 minutes). Set onions aside. Place an oiled rack over a roasting pan. Place livers on the rack and sprinkle with salt, pepper and thyme. Set oven rack at the second highest level. Broil livers for 5 minutes on one side. Turn livers and broil for 5 minutes on the second side. Discard juices from broiled livers. Combine livers and onions, and cool down this mixture until lukewarm. Into a food processor, place livers, onions and hard-boiled egg. Using pulse setting, process briefly until mixture is well blended. Avoid overprocessing so mixture still has slight texture. Taste for seasoning and add salt if needed. Spoon mixture into a serving bowl. Press egg yolk through a sieve and use to garnish. Serve with crackers or matzah. I like to spoon the chopped liver into one cup ramekins, which can be used immediately or frozen. The chopped liver can be frozen for three to four weeks.

Yield: About 2 cups of chopped liver

A Jew was walking on Regent Street in London and stopped in to a posh gourmet food shop. An impressive salesperson in morning coat and tails approached him and politely asked, "May I help you, sir?"
"Yes," replied the customer, "I would like to buy a pound of lox."
"No, no," responded the dignified salesperson, "You mean smoked salmon."
"Okay, a pound of smoked salmon."
"Anything else?"
" Yes, a dozen blintzes."
"No, no. You mean crêpes. Anything else?"
"Yes. A pound of chopped liver."
"No, no. You mean pâté."
"Okay," said the Jewish patron, "A pound of pâté. And I'd like you to deliver this to my house next Saturday."
"Look," retorted the indignant salesperson, "We don't *schlep* on Shabbos."

MOTHER'S CHICKEN SOUP

1 chicken (about 4 pounds) cut in eighths
2 tablespoons oil
2 onions, peeled and cut in quarters
3 carrots, peeled and cut in large chunks
3 stalks celery, cleaned and cut in chunks
3 small parsnips, peeled and cut in chunks
2 parsley roots, peeled and cut in chunks (See note below.)
8-10 cups water to cover
One bay leaf
1 teaspoon salt
3 tablespoons fresh parsley, chopped
3 tablespoons fresh dill, chopped

Heat oil in a 6-quart pot. Add chicken pieces and brown slightly on both sides. Add onions, carrots, celery, parsnip and parsley root. Add water to cover. Bring to a boil and skim the surface of frothy material. Add bay leaf. Cover and simmer for 2 hours. Add salt towards the end of cooking time. Strain broth. Reserve the rest of the chicken for another use. Chill overnight and remove congealed fat. Serve hot with noodles or kneidlach (matzah balls). Garnish each serving with a pinch of fresh chopped parsley and dill.

Yield: 8 to 10 servings

N O T E S : *Chicken fat which has been removed from the cooled chicken broth can be frozen and used in other recipes such as chopped liver or kasha varnishkes to give an authentic flavor.*

Parsley root is the actual root of the herb parsley. If available in the produce section of the grocery, it does add a nice flavor to the soup.

MATZAH BALLS (KNEIDLACH)

1 cup matzah meal
2 eggs, separated
1 cup boiling water
½ teaspoon salt
Dash of pepper
⅛ teaspoon nutmeg
1 tablespoon parsley, chopped
2 tablespoons chicken fat

Mix matzah meal, yolks and water. Add salt, pepper and nutmeg. Mix well.
Add parsley and chicken fat, and mix well again. In a separate bowl, beat
egg whites until stiff and fold into matzah mixture. Refrigerate for at least 30
minutes. Bring 2 ½ quarts of water to boil in a 4-quart pot. Form matzah meal
mixture into 1 ½-inch balls. Drop into boiling water and cook for 20 minutes.
Drain matzah balls and add to chicken broth just before serving.

Yield: 12 to 14 matzah balls

A new forestry graduate receives his first posting way out in the middle of a huge
forest with no people around for miles. Included in the survival gear that he's given,
much to his surprise, is a recipe for matzah balls. When he asks why he's receiving
a matzah ball recipe, he is told, "Sometime, a few years down the road, when the
solitude really starts to get to you, you're going to remember your matzah ball recipe.
You're going to get it out and start making some and, before you know it, you're
going to have ten Jewish women looking over your shoulder saying, 'That's not the
correct way to make matzah balls.'"

(And in the spirit of this little joke, I present one more recipe for matzah balls!)

NEVER-FAIL KNEIDLACH

2 eggs
¾ teaspoon salt
¼ cup vegetable oil
¼ cup water
¾ cup matzah meal
1 tablespoon chopped parsley (optional)

Beat eggs with salt. Mix in oil and water. Stir in matzah meal and parsley. Refrigerate one hour. In four-quart pot, boil 2 ½ quarts of water. Wet hands and form 10-12 balls. Drop into boiling water. Cook covered for 30 minutes (no peeking!). Drain with slotted spoon and serve in hot soup.

Yield: 10 to 12 kneidlach

Reprinted with permission of the Philadelphia *Jewish Exponent*.
Recipes by Fannie Fertik. Copyright 1985, by The Jewish Exponent, Inc.

TISHRI

KASHA VARNISHKES
(KASHA WITH BOW TIE NOODLES)

1 cup medium kasha
1 egg, beaten
2 cups boiling water
3 tablespoons chicken fat or oil
2 medium onions, peeled and diced
8 ounces sliced fresh button mushrooms
½ teaspoon salt
2 cups large bow tie egg noodles
Salt and pepper to taste

In a large heavy-bottom pot, mix kasha and beaten egg. Cook on medium heat, stirring constantly until the grains become dry and separated (about 2-3 minutes). Carefully pour boiling water over kasha and cover pot, allowing kasha to steam 5 minutes on low heat until the water is absorbed. Remove from heat and set aside.

Heat chicken fat or oil in a large skillet. Add onions and sauté until clear. Add mushrooms and sauté until tender.

In a 4-quart pot boil 2 ½ quarts of water with ½ teaspoon of salt. Add bow tie noodles, boil until *al dente* and drain. Gently toss kasha with onions, mushrooms and bow ties. Adjust salt and pepper to taste.

Yield: Serves 6 to 8. For more than 8 people, recipe can be doubled. It may also be prepared ahead of time and frozen. Kasha is also delicious added to chicken broth.

What are tefilin? Phylacteries. So what are phylacteries?
What is Kasha? Buckwheat groats. So what are buckwheat groats?

BARBECUED BRISKET

4-4 ½ pound brisket
Flour for dredging (about ½ cup)
3 tablespoons vegetable oil
Garlic powder
1 tablespoon sweet relish
1 (12-ounce) bottle chili sauce
3 medium onions, chopped
12 ounce can of beer

Place flour on waxed paper and coat brisket on all sides with flour. Heat oil in a large heavy-bottom ovenproof pan. Brown brisket on all sides on moderately high heat. Sprinkle both sides lightly with garlic powder while browning. Cover meat with relish, chili sauce, and onions. Pour beer around meat. Cover tightly. Cook at 300 degrees for 4 hours. Trim all fat. Slice against the grain and serve with its own gravy.

Yield: 8 to 10 servings

VARIATION (FOR SHREDDED BARBECUED BEEF):
Cut cooked brisket against the grain into 2-inch slices. Shred and serve with gravy in small dinner rolls.

QUICK APPLE CAKE

1 cup diced apples
¾ cup sugar
⅓ cup oil
1 egg, beaten
¼ cup orange juice
1 teaspoon grated lemon peel
1 ½ cups flour
½ teaspoon salt
1 teaspoon baking powder
1 teaspoon baking soda
1 teaspoon cinnamon
½ teaspoon vanilla
½ cup raisins

Preheat oven to 350 degrees. Grease an 8-inch square cake pan.

Combine diced apples and sugar, and allow mixture to stand for 10 minutes. Beat oil, egg, orange juice and lemon peel, and add to apple mixture. Combine flour, salt, baking powder and cinnamon, and add to the apple mixture. Stir in vanilla and raisins.

Pour into the prepared pan. Bake at 350 degrees for 35-40 minutes until a cake tester or knife comes out clean. Cool thoroughly on a rack, and cut into squares to serve.

Yield: 6 servings

On Rosh Hashanah, Jews cast pieces of bread into a stream or running body of water to symbolize the sinful acts they are discarding for the new year. For complex sins? Multigrain. For sins of the flesh? French bread. For sins committed in Seattle? Coffee cake. For sins committed in Philadelphia? Cheesecake. For sins committed in New York? Jewish Apple Cake.

JEWISH APPLE CAKE

When I was on faculty at Temple University in the Department of Ophthalmology, we would often share recipes in this multi-ethnic part of Philadelphia. At one of our luncheons, I tasted an excellent Jewish apple cake baked by one of our technicians Annamarie. Annamarie lives in South Philadelphia and is of Italian-American descent, which goes to show that you don't have to be Jewish to make great Jewish food! The term "Jewish" apple cake refers to the use of oil instead of butter as the shortening component of the cake, thus allowing this parve cake to be served after a meat meal.

FOR THE APPLES:
6 apples (I use 3 Granny Smith and 3 Golden Delicious apples.)
Juice from ½ lemon
½ cup sugar
1 teaspoon cinnamon

FOR THE BATTER:
4 large eggs
2 cups sugar
3 cups sifted flour
3 teaspoons baking powder
⅛ teaspoon salt
1 cup corn oil
¼ cup orange juice
2 teaspoons vanilla extract

Preheat oven to 350 degrees. Grease a large 10-inch tube pan (4 inches deep) with a removable bottom.

Peel, core and slice the apples. Cut each apple into quarters and each quarter into 4 pieces, yielding a total of 16 slices per apple. Sprinkle sliced apples with lemon juice to prevent discoloration. Mix sugar and cinnamon, and toss with apples. As the apples sit in the sugar mixture, they will exude juices. These juices should be drained off before apples are placed in the batter. Set apples aside.

In the bowl of an electric mixer beat the eggs for 2 minutes. Add the sugar slowly and beat for several minutes until the mixture is light yellow. In another bowl, combine flour, baking powder and salt, and blend with a fork. Alternately add these dry ingredients with the oil, orange juice and vanilla, and beat until smooth. This will be a very thick batter. Pour half the batter into the prepared pan. Place the apple slices over the batter, overlapping in a circular pattern. Avoid having the slices touch the side of the pan as this will cause the cake to stick to the pan and make removal more difficult. Pour the remaining batter over the first layer of apples. Place a second layer of apples in a similar circular pattern. There will be apple slices left over, and they make a delicious snack or dessert.

Bake at 350 degrees for 1 ½ hours. The cake is done when a cake tester or knife placed in the center of the cake comes out clean. After the cake has cooled on a rack, run a knife around the center and sides of the cake. Lift the cake up by the center tube. Then run a knife under the bottom of the cake to loosen it from the pan. Carefully remove the cake from the bottom of the pan with two spatulas and place it on the serving plate.

Yield: 16 servings

HONEY CAKE

Honey cake is the fruitcake of Jewish cuisine—often served but seldom savored. This dessert is traditionally served at the New Year table because honey symbolizes the hope for a sweet year ahead. I like this recipe because the addition of crushed pineapple brightens the flavor of the cake, and avoids the cloying sweetness present in some recipes. When the cake is completely cooled, I cut it into 2 x 2-inch squares and arrange the pieces in a single layer on an attractive serving plate. I then dust the pieces very lightly with confectioners' sugar.

½ cup (one stick) parve margarine (or butter) at room temperature
½ cup sugar
1 large egg
2 ½ cups sifted flour
1 ½ teaspoons baking soda
½ teaspoon baking powder
½ teaspoon salt
1 ½ teaspoons cinnamon
¼ teaspoon ground nutmeg
1 cup honey
1 cup hot decaffeinated coffee
1 ½ teaspoons vanilla extract
¼ teaspoon grated orange peel
¾ cup chopped walnuts (or pecans)
½ cup raisins
½ cup crushed pineapple, drained
2 tablespoons confectioners' sugar for dusting (optional)

Preheat oven to 350 degrees. Grease a 13 x 9 x 2-inch rectangular heat-resistant glass baking dish.

Beat margarine (or butter) in the large bowl of an electric mixer on medium speed until creamy. Add sugar slowly and beat until fluffy. Add the egg and beat for 3 minutes until the mixture is light yellow. Sift together flour, baking soda, baking powder, salt, cinnamon and nutmeg into another bowl. Combine honey, hot coffee, vanilla and orange peel in a heat-proof glass measuring cup, and stir to blend in the honey. With the mixer on low speed, alternately add wet and dry ingredients to the egg mixture and beat until smooth. Be sure to scrape down the sides and bottom of the bowl several times in between additions. Fold in nuts, raisins and crushed pineapple. Pour into prepared pan and bake at 350 degrees for 40-45 minutes until a cake tester comes out clean. Cool cake completely and slice into squares measuring about 2 x 2-inch. Arrange squares in a single layer on a serving plate. Place confectioners' sugar in a sifter or sieve, and lightly dust cake pieces if desired.

Yield: 24 pieces

BREAKING THE FAST

Yom Kippur is one of two fast days that are prescribed as full fasts (the other is the midsummer fast called Tisha B'Av). In contrast to the Fast of Esther, for example, on which observant Jews fast only from daylight to dark, fasting on Yom Kippur begins the night before the holiday and extends to complete darkness the following day. This can mean more than twenty-four hours without a morsel of food or a sip of water! The operative word, then, following the final blast of the shofar, is FAMISHED. The break fast is generally a dairy meal.

As Yom Kippur concludes, we look forward to Sukkot. It is traditional to hammer the first nail into the Sukkah at the end of Yom Kippur, and this is often done on a chilly dark night. OK, OK, I know you're hungry, so I'll stop chattering. LET'S EAT!

MENU *for* BREAKING THE FAST

Bagels

•

Cream Cheese and Butter

•

Nova Lox

•

Smoked Whitefish

•

Baked Salmon

•

Eggplant Bake

•

Tuna Salad with Walnuts and Cocktail Onions

•

Peaches and Cream Panna Cotta

•

Rick's Noodle Kugel

•

Schnecken

•

Coconut Pound Cake

•

Poppy Seed Cake

•

Coffee and Tea

EGGPLANT BAKE

When we lived in Louisville, Kentucky, we were fortunate to be invited to the elegant home of our friends Thelma and Aaron for Break the Fast. Thelma sets a beautiful table and is a superb cook. I have included three of her recipes in this chapter: eggplant bake, tuna salad with walnuts and cocktail onions, and coconut pound cake. The following is a cozy dish that definitely qualifies as "comfort food".

2 large eggplants
1 (10 ¾-ounce) can cream of mushroom soup
¾ cup Colby or mild cheddar cheese cut into small cubes
2 tablespoons butter
¾ cup crushed cracker crumbs

Preheat oven to 350 degrees.

Pierce eggplants in 2 or 3 places and bake on a greased cookie sheet for about 40 minutes until, when a knife is inserted, the centers are soft. Peel skin away and discard. Cut the eggplant meat into small cubes and place in a mixing bowl. Add mushroom soup and blend well. Add cheese and blend. Pour eggplant mixture into a greased baking dish. Heat butter in a medium sauté pan. Add crumbs and toss lightly until slightly golden. Watch carefully so they don't burn. Spoon crumbs over casserole and bake uncovered at 350 degrees for 30 minutes.

Yield: 6 to 8 servings

TUNA SALAD WITH WALNUTS
AND COCKTAIL ONIONS

4 (5-ounce) cans best quality tuna, drained
2 tablespoons lemon juice
4 tablespoons mayonnaise
2 stalks celery, diced
1 small jar cocktail onions, drained
½ cup walnut pieces

Blend tuna, lemon juice, and mayonnaise. Add celery, onions, and walnuts.
Blend together, and chill before serving.

Yield: 6 to 8 servings

PEACHES & CREAM PANNA COTTA

This is an updated version of a gelatin mold. By using unflavored gelatin and adding in the flavors, this recipe is refreshing and not overly sweet. It is made in two layers — a clear fruit layer and a cream layer. Use a blender for the second half of the recipe.

Spray a 5-6 cup gelatin mold with vegetable cooking spray.

FOR THE FRUIT LAYER:
1 (15-ounce) can of sliced peaches in heavy syrup
1 envelope unflavored gelatin
½ teaspoon grated orange peel

FOR THE CREAM LAYER:
12 ounces cream soda
1 envelope unflavored gelatin
4 ounces cream cheese at room temperature
4 ounces sour cream
¼ cup granulated sugar
¼ teaspoon almond extract
¼ teaspoon vanilla extract

Drain peaches and reserve the syrup. Add enough water to the syrup to make 1 cup. Sprinkle gelatin over syrup and mix. Microwave on high for 45 seconds and stir again to be sure all gelatin crystals are dissolved. Slice peach pieces in half. Add peaches and orange peel to the syrup mixture. Pour peach mixture into mold and chill for at least 3 hours.

Pour cream soda into a bowl. Sprinkle unflavored gelatin over the soda and mix to dissolve crystals. In a blender place the cream cheese and sour cream with ½ cup of the cream soda, and blend for 10 seconds. Then pour the remaining cream soda, the sugar and the almond and vanilla extracts into the blender with the cheese mixture, and blend until smooth. Transfer this mixture into a microwave-safe container. Partially cover with plastic wrap and heat in the microwave for 1 ½ minutes to be sure all gelatin crystals are dissolved. Allow cream mixture to cool down to room temperature. When fruit layer is firm, pour cream mixture over the fruit layer and chill for at least 4 hours. When firm, run a knife around edges of mold. Dip bottom of mold in a bowl of warm water. Unmold and serve.

Yield: 8 to 10 servings

RICK'S NOODLE KUGEL

Rick is a Philadelphia friend and fellow "foodie" who makes an excellent kugel. This is his recipe.

FOR THE NOODLES:
½ pound medium egg noodles
½ teaspoon salt
2 ½ quarts boiling water
6 tablespoons melted butter

FOR THE FILLING:
6 eggs, separated
½ cup sugar
6 ounces cream cheese at room temperature
4 tablespoons sour cream
1 pound small curd cottage cheese
1 cup golden raisins

FOR THE TOPPING:
3 teaspoons sugar
⅔ cup graham cracker crumbs (about 4 whole crackers)
2 tablespoons butter, melted

Preheat oven to 350 degrees. Grease a 13 x 9 x 2-inch ovenproof glass baking dish.

Cook noodles in salted boiling water until just *al dente*. Add melted butter to hot noodles and set aside. In the large bowl of an electric mixer, beat egg yolks well. Add sugar and cream cheese, and beat until smooth. Fold sour cream, cottage cheese and raisins into egg mixture. Then gently fold in noodles. Beat egg whites until stiff and fold into noodle mixture. Pour into prepared baking dish. Mix topping mixture until well blended and sprinkle evenly over top. Bake uncovered at 350 degrees for one hour until golden brown on top.

Yield: 10 to 12 servings

SCHNECKEN

Schnecken means "snails" in German. The spiral shape that is formed by the rolled layers of dough and filling mimic the elegant curves of the snail's shell. This is a delightful "pick-up" dessert that's sure to please. Making it is fun because it combines the ease and convenience of the food processor with the sense of accomplishment that comes from working with rolled-out dough. This dough is easy to work with as long as it is chilled.

FILLING:
½ cup brown sugar
½ cup pecans
½ cup golden raisins
3 tablespoons flaked, sweetened coconut
½ teaspoon cinnamon
½ cup dried apricots
3 tablespoons candied ginger

Process the brown sugar, nuts, raisins, coconut, cinnamon, apricots and ginger in the processor with the steel blade until it reaches the consistency of coarse grains. Any leftover filling freezes well for several months. Then wash and dry processor in order to make the dough.

DOUGH:
1 ½ cups flour
1 ½ teaspoons baking powder
1 stick unsalted butter, cold and sliced into pats
1 egg
¼ cup cold milk

Preheat oven to 350 degrees. Lightly oil four miniature muffin pans. Each pan will contain 12 schnecken.

Place flour, baking powder and butter in the processor and process with metal blade for 5 seconds. Add milk and egg and process for a few more seconds until a ball is formed. If you don't have a processor, cut butter into dry ingredients with two knives or a pastry blender until well blended. Then add the egg and milk to form a ball. Divide the dough into two equal parts and wrap in lightly floured plastic wrap. Then chill the dough in the freezer for 15 minutes or in the refrigerator overnight.

ASSEMBLY:
Dough, divided into 2 parts
Filling
½ stick unsalted butter, melted

Form the 2 parts of dough into 2 balls. Roll out the first ball on a well-floured board into a rectangle measuring about 9 x 12 inches. Spread half of the chopped ingredients evenly over the rolled dough. Drizzle ⅛ cup (¼ stick) melted butter over the filling. Roll the long side of the dough over itself, and continue rolling to form a jellyroll shape. Cut roll in half, then quarters, then eighths. Then cut each eighth into three slices for a total of 24 pieces for the first roll. Place each slice in one small greased muffin cup with the sliced side up to show the spiral shape of the dough. The first roll will fill 2 muffin pans. Bake the first two pans while you roll and slice the second roll. Bake at 350 degrees for 12-15 minutes. Check at 12 minutes and do not overcook. When schnecken are just beginning to turn golden, remove pans from oven and immediately turn out onto a cookie sheet to cool. These schnecken will freeze well.

Yield: 48 pieces

COCONUT POUND CAKE

2 cups sugar
1 cup solid vegetable shortening
5 whole eggs
2 cups flour
1 ½ teaspoons baking powder
1 teaspoon salt
1 cup buttermilk
1 ½ teaspoons coconut extract
1 cup sweetened, flaked coconut

GLAZE:
1 cup sugar
½ cup hot water
1 teaspoon coconut extract

Preheat oven to 350 degrees. Grease a large tube pan, 10-inch (4 inches deep).

Cream sugar and shortening. Add 5 eggs, one at a time, and beat well. Sift flour, baking powder, and salt. Add dry ingredients to egg mixture, alternating with buttermilk. Add coconut extract. Fold in coconut. Bake at 350 degrees for 50-55 minutes.

For glaze, stir sugar and water over low heat until sugar dissolves. Then boil for 1 minute and add coconut extract. While cake is still hot and in the cake pan, punch holes over top of cake and pour glaze over the cake, allowing glaze to run into holes. When cake is cold, remove from pan.

Yield: 12 servings

POPPY SEED CAKE

This is a terrific cake. It is easy to make and a big hit with everyone, including children, who seem to like the crunchy texture of the poppy seeds. I usually make this cake for Break the Fast, because my family requests it. However, poppy seeds are an ingredient typically found in desserts for Purim. Therefore, it can be part of your Purim repertoire as well.

4 eggs
1 box yellow cake mix
1 small (3.4-ounce) box instant vanilla pudding
½ teaspoon baking powder
½ cup oil
1 ⅓ cups hot water
1 teaspoon almond extract
4 tablespoons poppy seeds

Preheat oven to 350 degrees. Grease a 12-cup "Bundt" pan or a 10-inch tube pan (4 inches deep).

In the bowl of an electric mixer, beat eggs until light yellow. If cake mix appears lumpy, sift it or shake it through a strainer to eliminate the lumps. Add cake mix, pudding mix and baking powder and then beat. Add oil, water and almond extract and then beat once more. On low speed, add poppy seeds and beat briefly until all ingredients are well blended. Pour into the greased pan and bake for 45 minutes at 350 degrees until cake comes away from the sides of the pan or a cake tester comes out clean.

Yield: 12 servings

TISHRI

SUKKOT

Sukkot is that Jewish holiday most intimately associated with the earth itself, so there can hardly be a better time to celebrate God's bounties and beneficence. Shelter, hospitality and harvest are the themes of this magnificent celebration of life and ingathering.

Since this is one of those holidays which contains one holy day in Israel (and in Reform practice) but two outside Israel, let's detour for a moment in order to understand the reasons for this variation in Jewish observance.

This book began with a discussion of the moon and its central role as the key to understanding the Jewish calendar. The exact determination of the beginning of any month is naturally crucial because all the observances within that month are related to when it began. If we don't know what day Rosh Hashanah began, we can't know when Yom Kippur will be.

Without world almanacs and computers, how did anyone in ancient Israel know when the moon was "new"? The answer: When actual eyewitnesses said it was, and reported such to the Sanhedrin, the chief authority of law and practice. But, just as now, Jews lived in many other parts of the world besides Israel. There was a general understanding that nighttime took place in India before it took place in Jerusalem, but there was no exact worldwide calculation of the occurrence of the New Moon. Since our sages wanted everyone to celebrate the New Moon and the festivals at the same times as they were celebrated in Jerusalem, the solution was obvious. If Jews outside Israel extended their celebration for two days, it would be a certainty that all Jews would be celebrating our holidays at the same time they were celebrated there.

Now let's enjoy this amazing holiday. To do so, we have to build a *sukkah* and dwell in it. We have to obtain four specific things that come from the earth — palm branch *(lulav)*, willow *(aravah)*, myrtle *(hadas)*, and citron *(etrog)*. We also have to welcome guests. We even welcome imaginary guests *(ushpizin)* like Abraham, Jacob, Sarah or Leah — and give them an honored place in our *sukkah*.

What does the *sukkah* mean? That life is fragile, indeed. But there's so much more. After all, a *sukkah* can be made of so many different things, and it can even have one permanent side. But one thing about a *sukkah* — it has to be open to the sky. When we are in the *sukkah*, there is nothing between us and God. In addition, the *sukkah's* walls are not solid, but usually just a few pieces of wood or other material rather loosely constructed. As such, the wind and the rain that often come during this season do not affect it as they might a solid temporary structure. It's like a reminder of the fact that, if we can bend and be flexible, we have a better chance of standing up to life's storms and stresses.

Let me invite you into my *sukkah*. Have a seat. Oops, careful of Father Jacob over there. He's reaching for some soup. And, as we all know, it's not a good idea to fool around with Jacob when he's serving the soup!

SUKKOT LUNCHEON

Artichoke Quiche

•

Tuna Salad

•

Sliced Cucumber and Tomato Salad

•

Cheese and Crackers

•

Zucchini Walnut Bread

•

Pumpkin Cranberry Bread

•

Oatmeal Lace Cookies

•

Fresh Pineapple Chunks

•

Apple Cider, Tea or Coffee

ARTICHOKE QUICHE

1 unbaked (9-inch) deep-dish pie shell (from the freezer section at the grocery)
2 (6-ounce) jars marinated artichoke hearts
1 tablespoon vegetable oil
1 small onion, diced
1 garlic clove, crushed
4 eggs
½ cup half-and-half cream
¼ cup bread crumbs
⅛ teaspoon oregano
4 ounces sharp Cheddar cheese, shredded
2 tablespoons parsley, chopped fine
Salt and pepper to taste

Preheat the oven to 400 degrees.

Bake the pie shell for 10 minutes. Remove from oven and place on a rack to cool. Drain the artichokes, reserving the marinade. Sauté the onion and garlic in 1 tablespoon of the reserved marinade and 1 tablespoon of oil until onions are translucent. Whisk the eggs and cream in a bowl until blended. Stir in the bread-crumbs and oregano. Add the artichokes, onion mixture, cheese, parsley, salt and pepper. Pour into the pie shell and bake for 45 minutes. Serve warm.

Yield: 6 to 8 servings

Note: I usually double this recipe, so that I have an extra quiche for the next day or for the freezer. Doubling the recipe is also economical since there are 2 frozen pie shells in each package and the finely shredded Cheddar comes in 8 ounce bags in the dairy case.

TUNA SALAD

4 (5-ounce) cans best quality tuna, thoroughly drained
¼ cup mayonnaise
1 tablespoon fresh lemon juice
2 teaspoons sweet relish
½ teaspoon sugar
3 celery stalks, chopped fine

Blend all ingredients and serve on a bed of Romaine lettuce.

Yield: 6 to 8 servings

RED LENTIL SOUP PLUS

In the book of Genesis we read of Esau's giving up his birthright for a bowl of red pottage. Commentators suggest that this tempting dish consisted of red lentils since tomatoes and peppers were not available in Biblical times. In this soup I use red lentils for color and flavor, and a small amount of white beans and barley for flavor and texture. The soup is warming and delicious on a cold winter day, and one can imagine the ravenous Esau coming in from the hunt and craving it. I list chicken broth as one of the ingredients, but one can substitute vegetable broth for a totally vegetarian or parve soup. Last but not least, the healthful benefits of this dish are great, and the calorie count is low.

When working with dried legumes and beans, always remember to rinse them in a bowl of water, picking out any bits of sand or debris. Then, drain them thoroughly before adding to the soup. Since the cooking time for the white beans and barley is longer than for the lentils, I microwave the beans and barley, in order to avoid a soaking step. I take a 4-cup glass measuring cup in which I place 1 cup of water with the beans and barley together. I partially cover with plastic wrap and microwave on high for 4 ½ minutes. Then I drain these pre-soaked beans and barley and add them directly to the soup. The cooking time for dried lentils is much shorter than for dried beans and barley, and lentils do not require pre-soaking.

⅛ cup barley
⅛ cup dried navy white beans
1 cup water for pre-soaking beans and barley
3 tablespoons olive oil
1 medium onion, peeled and diced
2 carrots, peeled and diced
2 celery stalks, diced
1 small potato, peeled and diced
1 cup red lentils, rinsed and drained
1 large can (59-ounce) low sodium/low fat chicken broth
1 can (15-ounce) tomato sauce
1 can (15-ounce) water

Rinse barley and beans together. Place in a 4-cup heat-resistant glass measuring cup with 1 cup of water. Partially cover with plastic wrap and microwave for 4 ½ minutes to soften them.

Heat oil in 4-quart pot. Add diced onions, carrots and celery, and sauté for 2 minutes. Add the potato and continue to sauté. Add rinsed lentils and pre-soaked beans and barley, and blend. Add chicken broth, tomato sauce and water. Mix well and cover. After soup comes up to the boil, lower heat and allow soup to simmer, covered, on low heat for about an hour until white beans are tender.

Yield: 8 to 10 servings

STUFFED PEPPERS
WITH MEAT FILLING

TISHRI

For this recipe I use only red, orange or yellow peppers, which impart a delightful sweetness and avoid the slightly bitter taste of cooked green peppers. I use a 16 x 11-inch lasagne-type pan.

8 red, orange or yellow bell peppers

FILLING:
½ cup white rice
½ cup water for steaming the rice
1 ½ pounds lean ground beef
2 large eggs
¼ cup water for the filling
½ cup fine bread crumbs
1 teaspoon salt

SAUCE:
1 large onion, peeled and chopped
2 tablespoons oil
1 (28-ounce) can crushed tomatoes

TO PREPARE THE PEPPERS:
Rinse and dry peppers. Using a paring knife, cut around the top of each pepper and remove it. Reserve each top, which will be replaced on each stuffed pepper prior to cooking. With your hands, remove the white pith and seeds from inside the pepper and rinse clean. Trim away extra pith from each top. Lightly salt the inside of each pepper, and place each pepper in the pan.

FOR THE FILLING:

In a medium saucepan, steam the rice in ½ cup water until water is absorbed. At this point the rice will be only half cooked. Remove rice from the pot to a bowl and cool. In a mixing bowl, combine meat, eggs, ¼ cup water, bread crumbs, salt and cooled rice. Mix well. Fill each pepper ¾ full with stuffing and replace the top back on each pepper.

FOR THE SAUCE:

In a saucepan sauté the chopped onion in the oil. Add the crushed tomatoes and simmer on low heat 5 minutes. Pour the sauce over the peppers and cover tightly with foil wrap. Bake at 350 degrees for 1 ½ hours. Serve peppers and sauce over white rice.

Yield: 8 servings

VEGETARIAN STUFFED PEPPERS

8 red, orange or yellow bell peppers
Sauce from previous recipe

FILLING:
1 (14-ounce) package extra firm tofu, cubed into ½-inch pieces
3 tablespoons oil for browning tofu
½ cup brown rice
½ cup water for the rice
2 large eggs, lightly beaten
½ cup pine nuts
½ cup seasoned bread crumbs
1 teaspoon salt
2 tablespoons chopped parsley

Use a 16 x 11-inch lasagne-type pan.

Brown tofu cubes in oil until golden brown. Set aside and allow to cool. Steam rice in ½ cup water until water is absorbed. Rice will be half cooked. Transfer rice from the pot to a bowl and allow to cool. In a mixing bowl combine tofu, rice, beaten eggs, pine nuts, bread crumbs, salt and parsley.

ASSEMBLY:
Prepare peppers and sauce as in previous recipe. Stuff peppers with vegetarian mixture and replace tops. Pour sauce over peppers and tightly cover with foil. Bake at 350 degrees for 1 hour and 15 minutes. Serve peppers and sauce with brown rice.

Yield: 8 servings

SLICED CUCUMBER AND TOMATO SALAD

2 English cucumbers
2 boxes grape tomatoes

DRESSING:
6 tablespoons olive oil
2 tablespoons red wine vinegar
2 teaspoons fresh lemon juice
½ teaspoon salt
⅛ teaspoon pepper
¼ teaspoon dried oregano
½ teaspoon Dijon mustard
⅛ teaspoon sugar

With a vegetable peeler, remove green skin from cucumbers in alternating strips so some green strips remain. Slice cucumbers in ¼-inch slices. Rinse and drain grape tomatoes, and slice each one in half. Whisk dressing ingredients together until well-blended. Spoon dressing over cucumbers and tomatoes and mix well. Serve chilled.

Yield: 8 to 10 servings

SWEET AND SOUR CABBAGE ROLLS FOR SUKKOT

SAUCE:
2 large onions, peeled and chopped
2 tablespoons vegetable oil
1 clove garlic, peeled and crushed
2 (28-ounce) cans crushed tomatoes
Juice from 2 lemons
⅔ cup brown sugar
½ cup dark raisins

FILLING:
½ cup rice
½ cup water for steaming rice
2 pounds of lean ground beef
½ cup water
½ cup flavored bread crumbs
½ teaspoon salt
½ small onion, minced
3 large eggs, lightly beaten

1 large head of cabbage (*I prefer Savoy cabbage because leaves are easier to separate, and the flavor and appearance are better than that of regular cabbage.*)

Use a 16 x 11-inch lasagne-type pan.

SAUCE:
Sauté onions in oil until clear. Add crushed garlic and sauté 1 minute. Add crushed tomatoes and stir. Add lemon juice, brown sugar and raisins. Simmer for 10 minutes. Turn off heat and set aside.

FILLING:

Bring ½ cup water to the boil in a small pot. Add the rice and give it a stir. Cover and steam the rice for 3 or 4 minutes until the water is absorbed. The rice will be half cooked. Scrape partially cooked rice into a bowl and allow it to cool. Mix ground meat, water, bread crumbs, salt, onion, eggs and cooled rice until smooth.

CABBAGE ROLLS:

Parboil head of cabbage 8 minutes in a large covered pot with several inches of water. Remove the cabbage from the pot and hold under cool, running water for easier handling. Core cabbage and separate leaves. After removing outer leaves, you may need to parboil the remaining portion of the cabbage a few more times so that the remaining leaves can be separated and will be soft enough to roll. Place 2 heaping tablespoons of filling for the large leaves, and 1 heaping tablespoon of filling for the smaller leaves at the edge of each leaf. Tuck in ends and roll. Arrange in one layer in baking dish, edge side down. Pour sauce over rolls. Cover tightly. Bake 1 ½ hours at 350 degrees.

Yield: 25 to 30 cabbage rolls depending on the size of the head of cabbage.

NOTE: *For a quick recipe of sweet and sour cabbage and meatballs, roll filling into meatballs. Omit the parboiling step and slice the raw cabbage into thin wedges. Place meatballs, sauce and cabbage wedges in baking pan and bake, covered, for 1 ½ hours at 350 degrees.*

FRUIT COBBLER

This recipe will make 2 pans of cobbler. These pans may be covered and frozen. Then, when all the summer fruit is gone, bring out one of these for a treat.

FILLING:
16 Freestone peaches
20 Italian prune plums, cut in half with pits removed
Juice of 2 lemons
1 cup sugar
4 tablespoons instant tapioca (for puddings and fruit pies)

TOPPING:
1 ½ cups flour
1 teaspoon baking powder
⅔ cup packed light brown sugar
3 tablespoons fine cornmeal
2 sticks unsalted margarine or butter cut into pieces (at room temperature)
Whipped topping for garnish

Preheat oven to 325 degrees.
Spray two 13 x 9 x 2-inch baking pans with vegetable cooking spray.

Place peaches in boiling water for 2 minutes and then remove with a slotted spoon. Hold each peach under cold, running water and remove the peel with a paring knife. Remove the pit and cut each peach into 8 slices. Add the halved plums to the peaches. Sprinkle lemon juice, sugar and tapioca over the fruit and mix lightly. Pour fruit mixture into two 13 x 9 x 2-inch baking dishes.

Place flour, baking powder, brown sugar and cornmeal on a large bowl. Blend dry ingredients. Add pieces of butter or magarine and cut into dry ingredients with a pastry blender or two knives until the size of coarse grain. Sprinkle over fruit. Bake uncovered at 375 degrees for 30 minutes or until topping is lightly browned. Serve with whipped topping.

Yield: 2 (13 x 9 x 2-inch) pans, each with about 8 servings

OATMEAL LACE COOKIES

Each year we invite the kindergarten students and their families from our synagogue to our sukkah. The children love these cookies and the Moms clamor for the recipe. The dough should be made a day ahead and chilled in order to avoid too much spreading of these buttery treats.

1 cup quick cooking oats
1 cup sugar
3 tablespoons flour
1 teaspoon salt
½ cup (1 stick) unsalted melted butter (not margarine)
1 teaspoon vanilla extract
1 beaten egg

Preheat oven to 325 degrees.
Line 2 ungreased cookie sheets with parchment paper.

Mix together oats, sugar, flour and salt. Add melted butter, vanilla and egg and blend together. Refrigerate dough overnight. Then take chilled dough and drop ½ teaspoon of batter for each cookie. Space cookies about 3 inches apart, because they will spread while baking. Bake at 325 degrees for about 11 minutes or until edges are golden brown. Allow to cool slightly on parchment paper until cookies firm up. While still warm, lift cookies off with a spatula and cool on racks. Cookie sheets and parchment may be reused as needed to complete baking the cookies.

Yield: About 35 cookies

MANDELBROT

Mandelbrot are twice-baked cookies. Different culinary cultures have their own "twice-baked" cookies — "mandelbrot" or "kamishbrot" in Jewish cooking, "biscotti" in Italy, "beschuit" in Holland, "biskotta" in Greece, etc. Whatever the tradition, they make a light and delicious dessert. Of course, the dough can be made ahead and chilled in the freezer for later use. And, if you're lucky enough to be invited to someone else's sukkah, you couldn't bring a better "sukkah-gift" than Mandelbrot, attractively arranged on a plate for your host or hostess.

3 eggs
1 cup sugar
3 cups flour
1 teaspoon baking powder
1 teaspoon baking soda
⅛ teaspoon salt
1 ½ teaspoons cinnamon
¾ cup vegetable oil
½ cup chopped raw almonds (with the skins on)
½ cup raisins (I use ¼ cup dark raisins and ¼ cup golden raisins)

Preheat oven to 350 degrees.

In the large bowl of an electric mixer, beat the eggs for 2 minutes. Slowly add the sugar to the eggs and beat until the batter is light yellow. In another bowl, mix flour, baking powder, baking soda, salt and cinnamon with a fork. Alternately add dry ingredients and oil and beat on slow speed until blended. Fold in almonds and raisins by hand. Dough should be sticky at this point. Transfer dough on to a floured board and gather into a mound. Cut dough into 4 equal parts. Form each part into a log and wrap in floured plastic wrap. Chill dough for 1 hour.

Remove two of the four logs from plastic wrap and place at least 3 inches apart on a greased cookie sheet. Flatten each log into a rectangle with rounded edges measuring about 2 ½ by 8 ½ inches. Bake at 350 degrees for about 15 minutes until bottom of loaf turns golden. Remove cookie sheet from the oven. Transfer one loaf to a cutting board and slice each loaf diagonally. Replace each slice, cut side up on the cookie sheet. Repeat slicing process with second baked loaf. Rebake cookies for 10 minutes. Remove from oven and cool on a rack. Repeat entire baking process with last two logs of dough.

Yield: About 32 full size cookies
N O T E : *I cut off the 8 short rounded ends and do not rebake them. These can be reserved for those who like softer cookies.*

Selected desserts from Tishri. These desserts are, clockwise from top, pumpkin cranberry bread, oatmeal lace cookies, mandelbrot, and schnecken.

PUMPKIN CRANBERRY BREAD

3 cups sifted flour
1 tablespoon and 2 teaspoons pumpkin pie spice
2 teaspoons baking soda
½ teaspoon baking powder
1 ½ teaspoons salt
2 ¾ cups sugar
1 (15-ounce) can pumpkin purée (*NOT* pumpkin pie filling)
4 large eggs
1 cup vegetable oil
½ cup orange juice
1 cup dried cranberries

Preheat oven to 350 degrees.

Grease three 4-cup (about 8 x 4 x 3-inch) loaf pans. Disposable pans may be used. This quick bread does not require an electric mixer.

Combine flour, spice, baking soda, baking powder and salt in a bowl. Combine sugar, pumpkin, eggs, oil and juice in a large mixing bowl. Beat until just blended. Add dry ingredients to pumpkin mixture and stir briefly until well blended. Fold in cranberries. Spoon the batter into prepared pans. Bake for 50-55 minutes in 350 degree oven until tester comes out clean. Cool 10 minutes in pans.

Yield: 3 (8 x 4 x 3-inch) loaves

SPICY BANANA BREAD

2 cups unbleached flour
1 teaspoon baking soda
¼ teaspoon baking powder
¼ teaspoon salt
½ teaspoon cinnamon
¼ teaspoon ground ginger
¼ teaspoon ground allspice
1 cup brown sugar, packed
⅓ cup granulated sugar
1 teaspoon vanilla extract
2 eggs, beaten with a whisk
4 ripe bananas, mashed (measuring about 2 cups)
½ cup butter, melted
1 cup chopped walnuts
¾ cup dried currants

Preheat oven to 350 degrees. Grease 2 (8 x 4 x 3-inch) loaf pans. This quick bread does not require an electric mixer.

Sift together flour, baking soda, baking powder and salt. Add cinnamon, ginger and allspice and blend dry ingredients with a fork. Whisk brown sugar, granulated sugar and vanilla into beaten eggs. Add mashed bananas to egg mixture and blend. Alternately add dry ingredients and melted butter to egg mixture and blend well. Add chopped walnuts and dried currants and blend. Pour onto 2 prepared loaf pans and bake at 350 degrees for 50 minutes or until a cake tester comes out clean.

Yield: 2 (8 x 4 x 3-inch) loaves

ZUCCHINI WALNUT BREAD

3 large eggs
2 cups sugar
1 teaspoon vanilla extract
3 ½ cups sifted flour
1 teaspoon baking powder
1 teaspoon baking soda
½ teaspoon salt
1 tablespoon ground cinnamon
½ teaspoon ground ginger
1 cup vegetable oil
3 cups shredded, unpeeled zucchini (approximately 3 small zucchini)
1 cup chopped walnuts

Preheat oven to 325 degrees. Grease two 4-cup (8 x 4 x 3-inch) loaf pans.

In the large bowl of an electric mixer, beat eggs for 3 minutes on medium speed. Slowly add sugar to eggs. Add vanilla. In another bowl combine flour, baking powder, baking soda, salt, cinnamon and ginger, and stir with a fork. On low speed, alternately add oil and dry ingredients until well blended. Fold in zucchini and walnuts. Pour into the loaf pans and bake for 1 ½ hours at 325 degrees. Loaves are done when a cake tester or knife comes out clean. Cool thoroughly on cake racks before turning out loaves and slicing.

Yield: 2 (8 x 4 x 3-inch) loaves

CHAPTER 2
CHESHVAN

CHESHVAN

With more than half of its days as holidays, Tishri is definitely the busiest month of our calendar! The following month, Cheshvan, has no holidays besides Shabbat and affords a welcome chance to catch our breaths and settle down to the rhythm of our daily lives. It's popularly called "Mar Cheshvan" translated as "Mr. Cheshvan". Tishri is rather a hard act to follow, so this is a diplomatic way of making "Mr. Cheshvan" feel more important! The title "Mar" is also thought to mean "bitter" (as in the Hebrew word "Maror", bitter herbs) because legend has it that The Flood began during the month of Cheshvan. Yet a third meaning of "Mar" is "drop" which may refer to the first rains, which fall in Cheshvan.

In the Babylonian language, the word "Cheshvan" means "eight". That's right — names of the Hebrew months are not Hebrew at all, but Babylonian — specifically Akkadian (the Babylonian dialect which developed into Aramaic). Early in the fifth century B.C.E., Nebuchadnezzar conquered Judea, destroyed the first Temple which had been built by King Solomon, and exiled our people to Babylonia. But far from languishing there, our people developed a rich and vibrant culture which eventually resulted in the development of the Babylonian Talmud. The use of Babylonian words for our months is a significant legacy of our time in that land.

SHABBAT

Though Cheshvan may not contain any special holidays, this month certainly contains our most important holiday, the one that comes every week. The Sabbath is traditionally regarded as more important than any other holiday except Yom Kippur (which derives its stature as the holiest day of the Jewish year only because it happens to be another Sabbath, the Sabbath of Sabbaths). The Sabbath is the structural and spiritual compass of our people, always keeping us on course both religiously and temporally.

The foods of the Sabbath are what we associate instantly with the holiday, along with the warm glow of candle lighting and the taste of Kiddush wine. The prayers of the Sabbath are definitely prescribed, but so are the meals, of which there are three: a festive Friday night dinner, a joyous Saturday luncheon, and a convivial dairy meal at dusk on Saturday (*S'udah Shlisheet*). This third festive meal is traditionally enjoyed between the afternoon and evening services which are followed by *Havdalah*.

The foods we savor on Shabbat are the stuff of folklore, myth and collective reminiscence. For example, it is traditional to serve two loaves of *challah* on Shabbat. This custom reminds us of the double portion of manna we were given when we wandered in the desert (Exodus 16:22-26). And how many jokes or semi-humorous remarks have you heard about chicken soup? Well, good advice may indeed be chicken soup for the soul, but I'd rather have the real stuff, with kreplach that delight the palate as though they were made in heaven!

MENU *for* SHABBAT

Chicken Broth with Kreplach

•

Whole Roast Chicken

•

Friday Night Rice

•

Fresh Cranberry Apple Casserole

•

Broccoli Florets

•

Challah

•

Easy Lemon Pie

CHICKEN BROTH
WITH KREPLACH

4 cups clear chicken broth
½ cup shredded cabbage
4 snow peas cut into slivers
½ small carrot cut into slivers
1-inch slice fresh ginger
1 teaspoon soy sauce
12 kreplach (recipe to follow)

Add cabbage, snow peas, carrots, fresh ginger and soy sauce to chicken broth. Simmer for 5 minutes. Remove ginger slice before serving.

Yield: 6 servings

KREPLACH

These meat-filled dumplings may be made ahead and frozen. In addition, using leftover meat such as brisket for the filling simplifies the whole process.

FOR THE DOUGH:
2 cups unbleached flour
½ teaspoon salt
2 large eggs
4 to 6 tablespoons ice water

FOR THE FILLING:
About 2 ½ cups cold leftover meat, such as brisket
2 tablespoons cold leftover gravy, if available
1 small onion, diced
1 garlic clove, crushed
1 tablespoon oil
1 beaten egg

For the dough, place flour, salt and eggs in the bowl of a food processor fitted with a steel blade. Process until the ingredients have the consistency of coarse grains. Add ice water, one tablespoon at a time, until dough forms a ball. Remove dough to a floured board and knead for 5 minutes. Allow dough to rest for 30 minutes at room temperature.

While the dough is resting, place meat and gravy in the processor and shred using the steel blade. In a small pan sauté onion and garlic in oil for one minute. Mix cooked onion and garlic into meat. Add beaten egg and blend.

Divide dough in half. Roll out first half of dough into a 9 x 12 inch rectangle. Dough is elastic, and will require vigorous rolling. Dough should be thin, about ¼ to ⅛-inch thick. Cut dough into 2 ½-inch squares. Place ½ teaspoon filling in the center of each square. With your finger, moisten the edges of two adjacent sides of the square with water. Fold one corner of the dough over the filling to make a triangle. Then, using the tines of a fork, press the edges together to seal the kreplach and give an attractive appearance. Repeat the same process with the second portion of dough. Place the kreplach in a single layer on a floured pan until ready to cook. At this point the kreplach may be frozen.

Boil kreplach in salted water for 15 minutes. Drain and add to chicken broth.

Yield: About 36 pieces

WHOLE ROAST CHICKEN

1 whole roasting chicken, about 4 to 4 ½ pounds
½ teaspoon salt
3 tablespoons olive oil
1 teaspoon garlic salt
⅛ teaspoon pepper
½ teaspoon dried oregano
½ teaspoon dried thyme
¼ teaspoon dried marjoram leaves
1 small onion, peeled and quartered
1 tablespoon lemon juice
⅓ cup white wine or ¼ cup dry white vermouth
¼ cup water

Preheat oven to 350 degrees.

Remove any giblets from inside cavity of chicken. Rinse chicken thoroughly.
Remove kidneys if present and rinse again. Season the cavity with ½ teaspoon
salt. Line a roasting pan with heavy duty foil. Place chicken breast side down.
Coat chicken with half of the olive oil. Season back with half of the garlic salt and
herbs. Turn chicken over and use remaining oil and seasonings to cover breast,
wings and drumsticks. Place quartered onion in cavity. Add lemon juice, wine
and water to the bottom of the pan. Baste as needed during the cooking process. Roast at 350 degrees for 1 ½ hours. Carve and serve with
pan juices.

Yield: 4 to 6 servings

CUMBERLAND CHICKEN

When we lived in Kentucky, we spent some wonderful weekends with friends at Lake Cumberland State Park. Our group would pack food and prepare delicious meals together. This recipe was one of the dishes I cooked up for our Cumberland retreats.

2 small chickens (2 ½-3 pounds each), cut in eighths
⅔ cup flour
3 tablespoons oil
2 tablespoons margarine
½ teaspoon salt
⅛ teaspoon pepper
¼ teaspoon oregano
½ teaspoon thyme
2 medium onions
1 clove garlic, crushed
Juice of one lemon
Peel of 1 lemon, cut in strips
½ cup water

Preheat oven to 300 degrees.

Lightly coat chicken with flour. Put oil and margarine in large frying pan. When hot, brown the chicken, skin side down. Season chicken pieces with salt, pepper, oregano and thyme. Turn chicken over and season other side. When browned, place chicken pieces in a large baking pan. In the same frying pan, sauté the onions and garlic. When onions are clear, add lemon peel, lemon juice and water and simmer for 1 minute. Pour entire mixture on chicken. Cover snugly with heavy duty foil. Bake 2 ½ hours at 300 degrees. Serve over rice with sautéed zucchini.

Yield: 8 servings

NEWLYWED CHICKEN

So easy, and good, too! And the recipe is simple enough even for the novice cook.

3 tablespoons vegetable oil
1 (3-3 ½) pound chicken, cut in eighths
½ cup bottled French dressing
½ cup apricot jam
1 envelope dried onion soup mix
⅓ cup water

Preheat oven to 350 degrees.

Line a roasting pan with heavy duty foil. Pour oil onto foil. Place chicken pieces skin side down. Season the pieces with half of the salad dressing, jam and onion soup mix. Turn chicken pieces over and season the top of the chicken pieces with the remainder of the dressing, jam and onion soup mix. Add water to the pan. Bake at 350 degrees, uncovered, for 1 ½ hours.

Yield: 4 servings

NOODLE AND RICE KUGEL

1 pound sliced mushrooms
6 tablespoons margarine
2 cups fine egg noodles, uncooked
1 cup sliced water chestnuts
1 cup cooked rice
1 envelope dried onion soup mix
2 cups boiling water

Preheat oven to 350 degrees. Grease a 13 x 9 x 2-inch baking pan.

Sauté mushrooms in 2 tablespoons margarine. Set mushrooms aside in a bowl. In the same pan sauté raw noodles in remaining margarine until light brown. Combine sautéed mushrooms, water chestnuts and rice with noodles. Stir onion soup mix with boiling water and pour over noodle mixture. Pour into prepared pan. Cover and bake at 350 degrees for 40 minutes.

Yield: 8 servings

FRESH CRANBERRY APPLE CASSEROLE

3 cups peeled, cored and sliced apples
2 cups whole raw cranberries
1 ½ teaspoons lemon juice
¾ cup sugar
1 tablespoon oil for greasing the pan

TOPPING:
1 cup quick cooking oats
1 cup chopped walnuts
¼ cup packed brown sugar
½ stick melted margarine

Preheat oven to 325 degrees. Grease a 2-quart casserole dish.

Place apples and cranberries in an oiled 2-quart casserole. Sprinkle with lemon juice and sugar. Lightly mix topping ingredients in a medium bowl. Pour topping over fruit. Bake uncovered for 1 hour at 325 degrees.

Yield: 8 to 10 servings

FRIDAY NIGHT RICE

2 cups water
½ teaspoon salt
1 cup long grain rice
2 tablespoons vegetable oil
1 medium onion, peeled and diced
2 stalks of celery, cleaned and diced
1 medium green bell pepper, cleaned, seeded and diced

Bring 2 cups of water to a simmer in a medium saucepan. Add salt and rice and stir gently. Cover and simmer on low heat for about 15-20 minutes until all the water is absorbed. Set aside. In a shallow pan, heat oil until hot. Add onions, pepper and celery, and sauté until tender but slightly crunchy. Salt to taste. Blend rice with sautéed vegetables. Serve with roast chicken and pan juices.

Yield: 4 to 6 servings

BROCCOLI FLORETS

1 bunch broccoli
2 tablespoons olive oil
¼ teaspoon garlic salt

Cut off bottom 2 inches of broccoli stems and discard. Cut off remaining stems and peel off tough outer skin. Cut peeled stems into bite-sized pieces. Cut florets into bite-sized pieces. Rinse florets and stems in a big bowl of water. If any insects are suspected, add 2 teaspoons of salt to the rinsing water to dislodge them (rinse once more in fresh water if salt water was used). Drain broccoli pieces and place in a covered saucepan with 2 inches of water. Bring to the boil and steam for 4 minutes. Drain broccoli in a colander. Add olive oil to the same saucepan over moderate heat. Add garlic salt to oil and add broccoli florets. Toss broccoli for 10 seconds, then turn out into serving bowl.

Yield: 6 servings

EASY LEMON PIE

2 tablespoons solid vegetable shortening
1 ⅓ cups sugar
4 large eggs
⅓ cup fresh lemon juice
1 frozen, regular size, ready-made pie shell (not the deep-dish size)
Non-dairy whipped topping

Preheat oven to 350 degrees.

In the bowl of an electric mixer, cream shortening and sugar on low speed. Add eggs one at a time, and beat on medium speed for 2 minutes. Reduce mixer to low speed and add lemon juice slowly to avoid splattering. Pour mixture into pie shell and bake for 35 minutes until filling is set. Serve with a dollop of non-dairy topping.

Yield: 8 servings

THANKSGIVING

Thanksgiving sometimes falls in Cheshvan, so I've included some ideas for that wonderful American holiday. After all, the word "*Todah*" — "thank you" — is among the first words we learn as children, and saying thank you is what an observant Jew does just upon awakening — "*Modeh Anee L'fanecha…*", "I am thankful that You give me life and breath and the gift of a brand new day." And one of our most central prayers, so important that we say it three times a day, is called *Hoda'ah*, which means "Giving Thanks". And of course it was the Pilgrims who conceived of America as "the new Israel", a land to which they were directed by the finger of God.

MENU *for* THANKSGIVING

Turkey with Gravy

•

Chestnut Stuffing

•

Cornbread Stuffing

•

Cranberry Mold

•

Favorite Sweet Potato Casserole

•

Fresh Green Beans

•

Dinner Rolls

•

Top Crust Apple Pie

•

Fruit Platter

•

Coffee and Tea

TIPS FOR PREPARING TURKEY

IMPORTANT TIPS FOR THE NOVICE COOK:

1. The quality of the turkey is important. I prefer a fresh turkey to a frozen one, and I order it from a reliable source at least one week ahead.

2. If you are using a frozen turkey, thaw it in the refrigerator for at least 2-3 days (depending on size) before cooking. Thawing slowly in the refrigerator will avoid having to leave the turkey at room temperature, which can lead to spoilage.

3. If the turkey is fresh, have the butcher remove any plastic or metal hooks from the turkey, if present. They can be difficult to squeeze and dislodge.

4. Be sure to remove packet(s) containing the giblets, neck and liver from the turkey cavity or neck area. More than one cook has roasted a turkey only to find paper or plastic-wrapped giblets left in place at the end of roasting!

5. Plan to have the roasting completed 30-60 minutes before dinner. This margin of time is important for 3 reasons:
   A) The turkey needs to rest for at least 30 minutes, depending on size, so that, during carving, slices hold together and juices don't run off.
   B) This margin of time gives you an opportunity to make gravy and clean up the roasting pan, pots and strainer, avoiding a major clean-up later on.
   C) Timing is important when making a big dinner. It is preferable to have the food waiting for the guests rather than vice versa.

6. Even though the turkey may come out of the oven 30 to 60 minutes before serving, I do not carve it until shortly before dinner. Carving too far ahead causes the slices to dry out and lose flavor.

7. I prefer not to put stuffing in the turkey cavity. Not doing so accomplishes four things:
   A) It eliminates the need for elaborate trussing;
   B) The turkey cooks more quickly;
   C) The chances of spoilage are reduced;
   D) Stuffing can be made a week ahead, placed in a freezer and oven-safe casserole, and re-heated on Thanksgiving Day.

8. Before the holiday, be sure to have on hand:
   A) Regular thickness foil and heavy duty foil;
   B) A properly sized roasting pan which fits in your oven;
   C) A sturdy rack for the turkey, which fits inside your roasting pan;
   D) Plenty of paper towels.

9. Regarding cooking time, I use 15 minutes per pound as a guideline. The turkey is done when the thigh joint moves easily and the juices run clear.

Continued on next page...

CHESHVAN

ROAST TURKEY WITH GRAVY

TURKEY INGREDIENTS:

1 turkey *(12-15 pounds for 6-8 people who are looking forward to leftovers the next day)*

4-5 tablespoons olive oil

½ teaspoon salt

1 ½ tablespoons seasoned garlic salt

2 teaspoons sweet Hungarian paprika

1 tablespoon dried oregano

1 tablespoon dried thyme leaves

1 tablespoon dried marjoram

1 cup water to add to the bottom of the roasting pan

GRAVY INGREDIENTS:

2 tablespoons olive oil

Neck and giblets from turkey (Set aside liver for another use.)

32 ounces good quality low sodium chicken stock

2 medium onions, peeled and cut in chunks

2 carrots, peeled and cut in chunks

2 celery stalks, cut in chunks

2 bay leaves

4 tablespoons cornstarch for thickening the gravy

⅓ cup of water to dissolve the cornstarch

Optional: 1 teaspoon Gravy Master® Seasoning and Browning Sauce for color.

PREPARATION OF STOCK FOR GRAVY:

Pour 2-3 tablespoons olive oil into heated, heavy-bottom 4-quart pot. Add neck and giblets and brown lightly on all sides. Add chicken broth along with onions, carrots, celery and bay leaves. Bring to a boil. Then reduce heat, cover and simmer on low heat for 1 hour. Set aside and use this stock later to make gravy.

PREPARATION OF TURKEY:

1. Preheat oven to 425 degrees.
2. Line roasting pan with 2 layers heavy duty foil.
3. Place turkey rack in roasting pan over foil.
4. Rinse turkey and turkey cavity with cold water, being careful to remove all giblet packets.
5. With a sharp paring knife, remove kidneys if present from back cavity area. If left in place, these can impart a bitter taste. Rinse cavity again.
6. Sprinkle ½ teaspoon of salt in turkey cavity.

7. Place turkey, breast side down, on rack.
8. Rub back and legs with 2-3 tablespoons olive oil
9. Sprinkle back and legs with half of seasoned garlic salt, paprika, oregano, thyme and marjoram.
10. Turn turkey so that breast side is up. Repeat process with olive oil to breast and wing area. Sprinkle with remaining garlic salt, spices and herbs.
11. Cover breast and wings loosely with a piece of regular thickness foil to prevent excessive browning of these areas early in the cooking process.
12. Place roasting pan in the oven.
13. Add one cup water to the bottom of the roasting pan.
14. Bake for 15 minutes at 425 degrees. Then lower oven temperature to 350 degrees and cook at a rate of 15 minutes per pound or until indicator pops up or juices are clear.
15. 45 minutes before cooking time is completed, remove regular thickness foil from breast and wing area to allow browning.
16. During cooking process, check roasting pan every hour and add water if needed. Baste turkey periodically with bulb baster.
17. When roasting is complete, remove roasting pan from oven. Allow turkey to rest 30-60 minutes, depending on size. When pan is sufficiently cool, lift turkey and place it on a carving board where it can continue the resting process until ready to carve.

PREPARATION OF GRAVY:
1. Place roasting pan with remaining pan juices over two burners. Strain stock prepared earlier and add to roasting pan. Discard vegetables and giblets.
2. Over medium high heat, scrape pan juices to blend with stock.
3. Mix cornstarch with ⅓ cup cold water until dissolved. Add to roasting pan and stir gently until slightly thickened.
4. Add Gravy Master®, if desired, to give deeper color.
5. When slightly thickened, carefully strain into a large saucepan (I do this in the sink to avoid the splattering of hot liquids.).
6. Gravy may now be kept on the stovetop in a saucepan and be reheated as needed.

Yield: 6 to 8 servings with leftovers for sandwiches

CHESTNUT STUFFING

The most challenging part of this recipe is preparing the chestnuts. They may be cooked and peeled 1-2 weeks before the holiday and frozen. Then, on Thanksgiving Day, they will be removed from the freezer, thawed and tossed with the other ingredients before baking.

2 pounds chestnuts
5 cups crushed unsalted crackers or matzah
8 ounce container non-dairy creamer
½ stick parve margarine, melted

Preheat oven to 350 degrees.

Rinse chestnuts. Prepare roasting pan by lining with foil. Place a chestnut on a cutting board with the flat side down. Make 2 right angle cuts (or cross cuts) through the brown shell. Repeat with all of the chestnuts. Place prepared chestnuts in roasting pan and add water to cover the bottom of the pan. Cover lightly with a second sheet of foil and roast at 350 degrees for about 20 minutes. At this time, chestnuts will be cooked. Now remove the pan from the oven. The shelling process is simple if done while they are still hot. Remove just a few chestnuts at a time, and keep pan covered with foil or dish towel while working. Discard any moldy or spoiled chestnuts.

Break chestnuts in halves and thirds. Crush unsalted crackers or matzah to a coarse consistency. Add creamer and melted margarine and toss. Add chestnuts and lightly toss. Bake 35 minutes at 350 degrees in covered casserole dish.

Yield: 8 servings

CORNBREAD STUFFING

3 tablespoons vegetable oil
1 medium onion, peeled and diced
2 carrots, peeled and diced
2 celery stalks, diced
1 (16-ounce) bag cornbread stuffing mix
½ teaspoon salt
½ teaspoon poultry seasoning
2 eggs, beaten
2 ½ cups hot water

Preheat oven to 350 degrees.

Sauté onion, carrots and celery in oil for about 5 minutes. Set aside.
Place stuffing mix, salt and poultry seasoning in a bowl. Add beaten eggs and toss lightly just to blend. Add water slowly while tossing lightly with a fork. Add enough water to get a moist, but not mushy, consistency. Combine vegetables with stuffing mixture and toss lightly. Place in oven-safe dish.

Bake covered at 350 degrees for 35 minutes.
Stuffing may be frozen 1-2 weeks ahead.

Yield: 8 servings

THANKSGIVING CRANBERRY MOLD

1 small package strawberry flavored gelatin
1 envelope unflavored gelatin
1 cup boiling water
1 (8-ounce) can crushed pineapple, well drained
1 can whole cranberries
⅔ cup minced celery
⅔ cup chopped walnuts or pecans

Dissolve strawberry and unflavored gelatins in boiling water. Simmer the drained pineapple for one minute and cool down to room temperature. Add pineapple and remaining ingredients to gelatin mixture. Pour into mold sprayed with vegetable cooking spray. Refrigerate overnight.

Yield: 12 servings

FAVORITE
SWEET POTATO CASSEROLE

6 sweet potatoes
½ stick margarine
¼ cup brown sugar
1 (8-ounce) can crushed pineapple with juice
¼ cup orange juice
Large marshmallows

Preheat oven to 350 degrees. Use a greased 13 x 9 x 2-inch baking dish.

Scrub sweet potatoes clean. In a large pot, cover unpeeled potatoes with cold water and boil for 25-30 minutes. The sweet potatoes are done when a sharp knife, inserted into the center of the largest potato, reveals a soft consistency. Run cooked potatoes under cold water and remove peel. While potatoes are still hot, combine them in a mixing bowl with margarine and mash with a potato masher. Add brown sugar, pineapple with juice, orange juice and blend. Place potato mixture in the baking dish and bake, covered, for 20 minutes. Then remove cover, top with marshmallows and bake 10 minutes more. Watch carefully so that the marshmallows melt but do not burn.

Yield: 8 servings

SWEET POTATO APPLE CASSEROLE

6 sweet potatoes
3 apples (Golden Delicious are nice for this recipe)
Vegetable cooking spray
½ cup orange juice
3 tablespoons lemon juice
¼ cup sugar
2 tablespoons brown sugar
½ teaspoon cinnamon

Preheat oven to 350 degrees. Use a 13 x 9 x 2-inch baking dish

Boil sweet potatoes until tender and remove skins. When cooled, slice into ⅓-inch slices. Peel, core, and slice apples. Spray baking dish with vegetable cooking spray. Place potatoes and apple slices in dish. Pour orange and lemon juices over potatoes and apples. Sprinkle with sugars and cinnamon. Bake uncovered at 350 degrees for 25 minutes.

Yield: 8 servings

FRESH GREEN BEANS

2 pounds green beans
2 tablespoons vegetable oil
½ teaspoon salt

Snap off ends of green beans or cut ends off with scissors. Rinse beans in a large bowl of cold water and drain. Place beans in a 4-quart pot with 2 inches of water. Cover and bring water to the boil. Steam the beans for 6 minutes and drain immediately in a colander. Pour oil into the same pot. Add beans back to pot and toss briefly. Turn out onto serving dish and sprinkle with salt.

Yield: 8 servings

TOP CRUST APPLE PIE

This is an easier version of homemade apple pie. I make it in a 13 x 9 x 2-inch rectangular glass baking dish with a single pie crust on the top only. I use the classic flaky crust recipe which has been printed for many years on the label of the Crisco® brand vegetable shortening package.

FOR THE SINGLE CRUST RECIPE:
1 ⅓ cups sifted flour
½ teaspoon salt
8 tablespoons (½ cup) solid vegetable shortening, chilled and cut into pats
3-4 tablespoons ice water

FOR THE APPLE FILLING:
6 apples, peeled, cored and sliced
2 tablespoons lemon juice
1 teaspoon freshly grated lemon peel
½ cup sugar
1 teaspoon cinnamon
2 tablespoons corn starch

FOR THE GLAZE ON THE CRUST:
1 beaten egg yolk
2 tablespoons sugar
¼ teaspoon cinnamon

Preheat oven to 350 degrees. Grease a 13 x 9 x 2-inch heat resistant glass baking dish.

Place flour, salt and shortening in a mixing bowl. With a pastry blender, cut shortening into flour until mixture has the consistency of small peas. Add water, one tablespoon at a time, while using a fork to gather the dough until it comes together in a mass. Press the dough into a ball and chill at least 30 minutes in plastic wrap dusted with flour.

Place apples in a bowl. Add lemon juice and lemon peel and toss. Mix sugar, cinnamon and corn starch in a cup and add to the apples. Toss again. Pour apple mixture into the baking dish.

Place chilled dough on a floured board and roll into a rectangle measuring about 9 x 12 inches. Transfer dough to baking dish by rolling it onto the rolling pin and unrolling it over the baking dish. Brush dough with egg yolk and sprinkle with sugar and cinnamon. Bake at 350 degrees for 40-45 minutes.

Yield: 8 servings

CHAPTER 3

KISLEV & TEVET

KISLEV & TEVET

DATES *of* THE JEWISH HOLIDAYS IN KISLEV

25-29 KISLEV:
FIRST FIVE DAYS OF CHANUKAH
OR
25-30 KISLEV:
FIRST SIX DAYS OF CHANUKAH

DATES *of* THE JEWISH HOLIDAYS IN TEVET

1-3 TEVET:
LAST THREE DAYS OF CHANUKAH
OR
1-2 TEVET:
LAST TWO DAYS OF CHANUKAH

10 TEVET:
FAST OF THE TENTH OF TEVET
Commemorating the Babylonians' breaching the walls of
Jerusalem when they laid siege to the City in 586 B.C.E.

Kislev, like Cheshvan, may contain twenty-nine or thirty days (Yes, this is a little complicated and beyond the scope of this book). It depends upon when the full moon occurs on the *following* Tishri. Oy, it's a real *megillah!* — but not to worry. The sages figured all this out centuries ago, and you can consult many references to find out the length of Kislev in any given year.

The word Kislev derives from the Babylonian, and conveys the meaning of trust or security. Some commentators have linked this meaning with the bravery and persistence of Judah Maccabee and his forces.

CHANUKAH

The celebration of Chanukah has evolved over many centuries, and we see the holiday today through the dual lenses of history and myth. The first narrative of Chanukah occurs in the Apocrypha (200 B.C.E. - 100 C.E), a group of books not deemed holy enough to be in the Hebrew Bible.

In the second century before the Common Era, Jews lived in Judea under the oppressive regime of the Greek-Syrians and their ruler Antiochus. In an attempt to be "progressive", Antiochus had adopted Greek or Hellenic culture — and he tried to force this on all the Jews in his realm. Many Jews, so-called Hellenists, complied, but others resisted. A struggle therefore began not only between Syrian and Jew, but also between Jew and Jew.

The dramatic beginning of the rebellion against the Syrians occurred in the small town of Modin, west of Jerusalem. A Jewish zealot named Mattathias watched in horror as a Jew knelt before a Greek idol. He drew his sword, assassinated the Hellenist, and with his sons (including the famous Judah Maccabee) began a fierce guerilla campaign against the Syrian army. By this time, Antiochus had taken control of the Temple in Jerusalem, instituting idol worship and the eating of pork within its walls.

The miraculous victory of the Maccabees in 165 B.C.E. was climaxed by the rededication (Chanukah in Hebrew) of the Holy Temple. About four centuries later, in the Gemara (part of the Talmud), our Rabbis further embellished the Chanukah story. There we are told of the miracle of the oil. When we reclaimed the Temple, we found enough oil to illuminate the Eternal Light for just one day. But this small amount of oil lasted for eight days until more could be obtained.

•

The traditional foods of Chanukah are hearty and rich — and very comforting against the early winter chill. Oil holds the starring role as the symbol of the miracle that occurred during the rededication of the Second Temple. For Ashkenazic Jews, potato *latkes* are the *sine qua non* of the holiday. One can also find oil-based recipes which are variations on the *latke* theme such as zucchini, carrot or apple pancakes. Because making *latkes* can be so demanding, I try to keep the accompanying recipes simple. The shredding attachment on my food processor makes grating the potatoes and onions a snap, and the baking powder prevents the potatoes from turning brown.

I serve the *latkes* with standing rib roast or slow-cooked brisket and applesauce. For a dairy or parve meal, sour cream is a delicious accompaniment.

In Israel and throughout the world, we also make jelly donuts (*sufganiyot*) to celebrate the holiday. Fried in oil, they are a wonderful dessert for the Chanukah meal. So, almost anything fried might be said to be "Chanukah-dikeh", to coin a phrase.

And speaking of coins, or *gelt* (from the Yiddish word for money), you may be wondering about those wonderful chocolate coins that we enjoy on Chanukah. After the Maccabees conquered the Syrians, their descendants, the Hasmoneans, began manufacturing coins depicting their leaders. We eat these chocolates today as a delicious reminder of the Hasmonean dynasty which governed our people for a century until about 37 B.C.E.

Another familiar and delightful symbol of Chanukah is the four-sided top called the *dreidel* (Yiddish for spinner or top). Some authorities believe that the Jews played such a game in order to fool Greek authorities who had forbidden them from studying Torah. Whatever its origin, this very old game of chance is played with a four-sided top, each side containing a Hebrew letter — *nun, gimel, hey,* and *shin.* The letters are the first words of the Hebrew words *Nes* (Miracle), *Gadol* (Great), *Hayah* (Happened), and *Sham* (There) — "A Great Miracle Happened There" (In Israel, incidentally, the *shin* is replaced with the letter *pey,* so the phrase becomes "A Great Miracle Happened Here"). A player spins the top and, if it falls on the side with the Hebrew letter *Gimel* facing up, the lucky winner wins all the money.

•

In the Chanukah tale, we are riveted by all of the elements of a great story: a powerful and oppressive ruler who is vanquished by the faith and bravery of the Maccabees; and the miracle of the oil, symbolizing the flame of our faith which will not be extinguished. This powerful combination continues to inspire us and fill us with awe every year. Whatever struggles our people may face in the future, the story fills us with joy and hope, and we celebrate the Festival of Lights with excitement and enthusiasm.

Here are some Chanukah words you might want to know:

- The nine-branched candelabrum which we use to display the Chanukah candles is called a *chanukiyah.* It may also be called a *menorah,* which is the word for any candelabrum.
- The Hebrew word for candle is *ner.* You can hear the sound in the longer word me*NOR*ah.
- Potato pancakes, called *latkes* in Yiddish, are called *l'veevot* in Hebrew.
- Jelly donuts are called *sufganiyot* in Hebrew.
- Someone who loves to eat all this stuff is called a *fresser* in Yiddish!

MENU *for* CHANUKAH

Standing Rib Roast Beef

•

Potato Latkes

•

Chunky Applesauce

•

Cucumber Salad

•

Family Fun Chanukah Sugar Cookies

POTATO LATKES

6 medium russet potatoes, peeled
½ teaspoon baking powder
1 teaspoon salt
4 tablespoons flour
2 eggs, beaten
1 large onion, peeled
Vegetable oil for frying (about 10-12 tablespoons)

Grate potatoes and onions with a hand grater or the shredding disc of a food processor. Add baking powder, salt and flour and blend. Add beaten egg.

Heat a heavy bottomed fry pan with 6 tablespoons of oil. Using a ¼ cup measure, scoop up potato mixture and drain off any excess liquid. Place the latke in the hot oil. Flatten the pancake with a spoon. Repeat until pan is full. Fry until first side is golden. Flip the latkes and brown the second side. Remove browned latkes and drain on paper towels. Repeat this process until all of the potato mixture is used up, adding additional oil as needed to the pan. Serve with applesauce or sour cream. Latkes can be set aside and gently reheated uncovered on a cookie sheet in a 325 degree oven for about 5 minutes before serving.

Yield: 18 to 20 Latkes

STANDING RIB ROAST

Roast beef always makes a big hit at a festive table. Paired with potato latkes, it is a sensational meal. I always buy the rib-in roast beef since someone always wants the bone.

One 2-rib standing rib roast at room temperature (weighing about 5 pounds)
3 tablespoons vegetable oil
4 tablespoons Worcestershire sauce (See page 201, number 7 regarding the dietary laws.)
1 tablespoon garlic salt
Pepper to taste
⅔ cup water

Remove roast from refrigerator 2-3 hours before cooking to bring it to room temperature for more even cooking.

Preheat oven to 425 degrees.

Line a roasting pan with heavy duty foil. Season all sides of roast with oil, Worcestershire sauce, garlic salt and pepper. Leave the roast in the rib up (fat side up) position. Add ⅔ cup water to the bottom of the pan. Bake at 425 degrees for 15 minutes and then turn oven temperature down to 350 degrees for the remainder of the cooking time. For medium doneness a cooking time of 25 minutes per pound works well. Add water to the bottom of the pan as needed, and this will form the *jus* to serve along with the beef at the table. Allow the roast to rest for a few minutes before slicing.

Yield: 6 servings

BEST BRISKET

Since making latkes for Chanukah is a fairly involved process, it's helpful to keep the rest of the meal preparation as simple as possible. This brisket recipe is so easy to make, and everyone likes it, even the picky eaters in my family.

2 tablespoons oil
3 ½-4 pound brisket (first cut brisket trimmed of fat)
Flour for dredging
1 cup barbecue sauce
1 envelope dried onion soup mix
⅔ cup water

Preheat oven to 275 degrees.

Heat oil in an ovenproof pan. Dredge brisket in flour, and brown on all sides. Coat both sides of meat with barbecue sauce and sprinkle both sides with onion soup mix. Add water to pan. Cover tightly with heavy duty foil or the pan's cover.

Bake in a 275 degree oven for 4 hours. When brisket is done, allow to rest for 15 minutes before slicing. Serve meat with its own gravy.

Yield: 6 to 8 servings

CUCUMBER SALAD

Preparing this refreshing salad a day ahead improves the taste and saves time when making dinner the next day.

¼ cup white vinegar
1 tablespoon lemon juice
1 tablespoon sugar
1 teaspoon salt
⅛ teaspoon pepper
¼ cup chopped onion
2 tablespoons parsley
4 medium cucumbers, peeled and halved lengthwise

Mix all ingredients except cucumbers in a glass jar or plastic container. Remove and discard the seeds from the cucumber halves with the tip of a teaspoon. (A grapefruit spoon works well for this task.) Cut cucumbers into 1/4-inch slices and toss with the dressing. Chill thoroughly. Turn or shake container several times while chilling. For best taste, chill overnight.

Yield: 4 to 6 servings

Reprinted with permission of the Philadelphia *Jewish Exponent*.
Recipes by Fannie Fertik. Copyright 1985, by The Jewish Exponent, Inc.

CHUNKY APPLESAUCE

8 apples, peeled, cored and cut into ½-inch dice
½ cup sugar
1 tablespoon fresh lemon juice
¼ cup orange juice
¼ teaspoon cinnamon

Combine all of above ingredients in a sauce pan. Bring up to the simmer and cook for 25 minutes. Serve with latkes.

Yield: 8 servings

APPLE FRITTERS

½ cup water
1 egg
2 tablespoons margarine, melted
Grated rind and juice from half an orange
½ cup of chopped apples
½ teaspoon vanilla extract
1 ½ cups cake flour
¼ teaspoon salt
1 tablespoon baking powder
Vegetable oil for frying (such as canola or peanut oil)
2 tablespoons confectioners' sugar

In a bowl, combine water, egg and margarine. Add grated rind and juice of orange, chopped apples and vanilla. Set aside.

Sift together flour, salt and baking powder. Stir flour mixture into liquids with a spoon until blended. Drop batter by spoonfuls into ½-inch hot oil. Fry to a golden brown on both sides. Drain on paper towels. Place confectioners' sugar in a fine sieve and dust fritters before serving.

Yield: About 24 fritters

FAMILY FUN CHANUKAH SUGAR COOKIES

I present two versions of this sugar cookie recipe. Making the dough and decorating the cookies are fun activities to do with children. The dough is quite stiff, and I use the dough hook and my standing mixer to mix up the dough. The flour should be added in at the lowest speed. Once the flour is incorporated, medium speed should be used until the dough forms a ball. The first version is delicious and very easy to make. After the dough is made, chilled and sliced, decorating the cookies will bring out the creative side of young cooks. Decorations can vary from colored sugar, chocolate sprinkles, multi-colored sprinkles or slivers of drained maraschino cherries.

The second version for rolled cookies is a bit more ambitious. Because the dough is rich in shortening, I divide it into four parts for chilling. I then roll it out in small batches, keeping the remaining dough chilling in the fridge for easier handling.

FOR EASY SLICED SUGAR COOKIES:

½ pound (2 sticks) unsalted margarine or unsalted butter (room temperature)
½ cup sugar
1 teaspoon vanilla extract
1 egg yolk from 1 large egg
2 ½ cups flour
⅛ teaspoon salt
1 egg yolk beaten with 1 teaspoon water to use for decorating

FOR ROLLED SUGAR COOKIE DOUGH TO USE WITH COOKIE CUTTERS:

½ pound (2 sticks) unsalted margarine or unsalted butter (room temperature)
½ cup plus 2 tablespoons sugar
1 teaspoon vanilla extract
1 whole large egg
3 cups flour
¼ teaspoon salt
1 egg yolk beaten with 1 teaspoon water to use for decorating
Colored sugar or multi-colored sprinkles for decoration

Preheat oven to 350 degrees.

Cream margarine (or butter) and sugar together. Add vanilla and egg. Add flour and salt and blend with a fork to make a sticky dough (or use the dough hook attachment with the electric mixer). Wrap dough in floured plastic wrap. Chill thoroughly for at least two hours. After chilling, place dough on a lightly floured board. For round, sliced cookies, roll dough into a log and slice cookies ¼-inch thick. The sliced cookie should have a diameter of 2-2 ½-inches and a thickness of ¼-inch. Place cookies on ungreased baking sheet. Brush cookies with egg yolk wash and sprinkle with decorative blue sugar crystals or other decorations if desired. Bake 8-10 minutes at 350 degrees until the edges are slightly golden.

For rolled holiday shaped cookies, flour a board and rolling pin. Break dough into small batches and roll out dough to ¼-inch thickness. Use extra flour to dust board and rolling pin as needed to avoid sticking. Use cookie cutters shaped like a dreidel and a Star of David to cut out shapes. Dust edges of cookie cutters with flour after each cut to avoid sticking. As above, place cookies on a cookie sheet and brush cookies with egg yolk wash prior to decorating.

As above, bake cookies 8-10 minutes at 350 degrees.

Yield: 3 dozen cookies

CHAPTER 4

SHEVAT

SHEVAT

DATES *of* THE JEWISH HOLIDAYS IN SHEVAT

15 SHEVAT:
TU B'SHEVAT
OR
ROSH HASHANAH LA'ILANOT
(NEW YEAR OF THE TREES)

TU B'SHEVAT

Having the New Year fall in the seventh month is doubtless confusing enough — but suppose I tell you that our people really observe several New Years! It's true. There is the popular New Year that falls in Tishri, the Seventh Month. There is the legal New Year that begins with Nisan, the first month. And there is the New Year for the Trees, which falls on the Fifteenth of Shevat. The Hebrew letters signifying fifteen are *Tet* and *Vav* which may be vocalized as *Tu* — thus, Tu B'Shevat simply means the Fifteenth Day of the Hebrew month Shevat.

Trees are precious to our people. Jewish comedians tell of traveling to Israel, getting off the plane, and demanding to see the trees for which they donated money to the Jewish National Fund when they were children in Hebrew school. Trees, planted for decades in the Holy Land, have brought it water, shade, and life. In the words of the song, *"Etz kadosh"* — "a tree is holy, that's why a seed is like a prayer / Branching out in all directions, showing God is everywhere".

The tree is one of the most powerful symbols in Judaism. The Torah itself is a Tree of Life to those who hold it close. A tree is a central symbol of one of the earliest stories in the Bible. So, on this holiday, we plant trees and enjoy their fruit. Therefore, foods with fruits and nuts are typically served to celebrate this holiday. Although it is still winter in the United States, that first special hint of spring will soon be here. In Israel, Tu B'Shevat means that spring is really here, and the season of planting has begun.

There is an interesting modern connection between Chanukah and Tu B'Shevat, the holiday that follows it just six and a half weeks later. When you land at Ben Gurion Airport in Tel Aviv, you are just a few miles from Modin, the town in which the Maccabean rebellion began. If you take the twenty minute drive there, you will find one of Israel's most famous and beautiful forests, and your first "official" act on Israeli soil could be to plant a tree (or to find the one you sent money for years ago!). I recommend it!

MENU *for* TU B'SHEVAT

Pomegranate / Endive / Grapefruit Salad
•
Coconut Panko Fried Fish with Pineapple Salsa
•
Steamed Rice
•
Carrot Ring
•
Tu B'Shevat Treats
•
Heirloom Marble Cake

POMEGRANATE / ENDIVE / GRAPEFRUIT SALAD

5 tablespoons vegetable oil (such as canola oil)

3 tablespoons fresh lime juice

Grated peel of 1 lime

1 tablespoon honey

⅛ cup pomegranate juice (Seeds can be pressed or processed and strained
for fresh juice, or bottled juice may be used.)

¼ teaspoon salt

Dash of pepper

3 pink grapefruits

4 cups loosely packed Boston lettuce leaves, washed, spun dry and torn
into pieces

2 large Belgian endives, sliced crosswise in 2-inch sections

¾ cup pomegranate seeds

Whisk together oil, lime juice and zest, honey, pomegranate juice, salt and
pepper. Set aside. Peel and section grapefruits. Drain grapefruit sections and
reserve juice for another purpose. Toss lettuces with dressing and divide among
6 salad plates. Place 6 grapefruit sections over each serving of lettuce. Sprinkle
with pomegranate seeds and serve.

Yield: 6 servings

COCONUT PANKO FRIED FISH WITH PINEAPPLE SALSA

FOR THE FISH:
1 pound fish filets, such as flounder or tilapia
Salt
Pepper
Garlic powder
1 cup sweetened flaked coconut
1 cup panko bread crumbs
¾ cup flour
2 whole eggs, beaten
Vegetable oil for frying, about 6 tablespoons

FOR THE PINEAPPLE SALSA:
2 tablespoons vegetable oil
1 medium onion, chopped
⅔ cup diced green bell pepper
3 tablespoons brown sugar
2 cups fresh pineapple, cut into small chunks
2 tablespoons minced fresh cilantro

Rinse and pat dry fish filets. Sprinkle each filet lightly with salt, pepper and garlic powder. Mix coconut and panko together. Line up 3 bowls — the first containing flour, the second with beaten eggs and the third with the coconut/panko mixture. Take a filet and dredge it first in the flour. Then coat it on both sides with the egg, and finally coat both sides with the coconut/panko mix. Heat oil in a large frying pan. Add filets and fry on both sides until golden. Serve with pineapple salsa.

For the salsa, sauté the onion over moderate heat until clear. Add the green pepper and cook 3 more minutes. Remove onion and pepper and set aside. Place brown sugar and pineapple chunks in the same pan and sauté for 3 minutes. Add back onions and peppers to the pan and blend all ingredients for one minute. Serve the salsa warm or at room temperature, garnished with minced cilantro.

Yield: 4 to 6 servings

CARROT RING

This is a favorite recipe from friends in Louisville, Kentucky, where Rita and Patti ran a catering business.

½ cup butter at room temperature
½ cup brown sugar
2 eggs
5 large carrots, peeled and grated
Juice of 1 lemon
½ cup sour cream
¼ cup sifted flour
1 teaspoon baking powder
1 teaspoon baking soda
½ teaspoon salt

Preheat oven to 350 degrees. Spray a 10-inch tube pan with removable bottom with vegetable cooking spray.

Cream the butter. Add sugar and beat until fluffy. Add eggs one at a time, beating after each addition. Fold in grated carrots, lemon juice and sour cream. Add flour, baking powder, baking soda and salt to carrot mixture and blend all ingredients. Spoon the mixture into the greased tube pan. Bake at 350 degrees for 35-40 minutes until a cake tester comes out clean and the top is lightly puffed and golden. Remove from oven and allow the ring to cool. Run a knife around the sides and center of the pan and lift out the carrot ring. Cut in pieces and place on serving plate. Or, to serve the ring intact, run a knife between the carrot ring and the bottom of the pan. Then place two spatulas under the bottom of the ring, lift it up, and place it on a serving plate.

Yield: 10 to 12 servings

TU B'SHEVAT TREATS

Making these sweets is a fun activity which works best with one adult and two children. While the adult slices the fruit into halves, one child can assemble the treats and one child can wrap them. This treat is like a mini-sandwich, with a marshmallow half and a hazelnut enclosed between two halves of prune or two halves of apricot. For best results the dried fruit needs to be moist and fresh. Pecan halves cut in half can be substituted for the hazelnuts. If there is any question of nut allergies, as in a school setting, the nuts can be eliminated altogether.

24 large marshmallows, cut in half
48 hazelnuts (or 24 pecan halves cut in half)
24 pitted prunes, cut in half
48 dried apricot halves

Take one marshmallow half and one hazelnut and press the two together. Then enclose the marshmallow and nut between two prune halves and press the sandwich together. Wrap the treat in a square of plastic wrap and twist the ends to seal the treat. Repeat the process with all of the prune halves. Then do the same thing with the apricot halves. Pile the treats in an attractive bowl for presentation.

Yield: 48 pieces

HEIRLOOM MARBLE CAKE

This is a delicious butter cake from an old family recipe. The recipe calls for a whipped cream frosting, which is not too sweet and which complements the rich butter cake. I present two options for the pan size. For a simpler sheet-type cake a 13 x 9 x 2-inch heat-resistant glass dish or cake pan can be used. With this type of dish the cake can be cut into squares and served directly from the pan. For a circular cake like the one in the photo, use a 10-inch springform pan.

VANILLA BATTER:
3 cups sifted cake flour
3 teaspoons baking powder
½ teaspoon baking soda
¼ teaspoon salt
1 cup (2 sticks) unsalted butter at room temperature
2 cups sugar
4 large eggs
1 cup whole milk
1 teaspoon vanilla

CHOCOLATE FLAVORING FOR THE CHOCOLATE BATTER:
3 tablespoons unsweetened cocoa, sifted
2 tablespoons sugar
2 tablespoons whole milk

FROSTING:
2 cups whipping cream
1 cup confectioners' sugar
½ cup unsweetened cocoa, sifted

Preheat the oven to 350 degrees. For the rectangular cake, grease a 13 x 9 x 2-inch heat resistant glass dish. For the circular cake, grease a 10-inch springform pan and line the bottom with a circle of parchment paper cut to fit the bottom of the pan.

Sift flour with baking powder, baking soda and salt, and set these dry ingredients aside.

For the vanilla batter, cream the butter in the bowl of an electric mixer. Slowly add the sugar and beat until fluffy. Add the eggs one at a time, scraping down the sides in between additions. Alternately add the dry ingredients and the milk on low speed. Add the vanilla and beat.

For the chocolate batter, mix the cocoa, sugar and milk until smooth. Add this mixture to 1 cup of vanilla batter and mix until the chocolate is evenly distributed.

Into the prepared pan pour about ¼ of the vanilla batter. Then add a dollop of the chocolate batter next to the vanilla batter. Repeat this until both batters are used up and the bottom of the pan is covered. Do not mix the batters, as they will blend during the baking process.

Bake at 350 degrees. For the rectangular pan, the baking time is 40-45 minutes. For the circular pan, the baking time is an hour. The cake is done when a cake tester or sharp knife placed in the center of the cake comes out clean, or when the cake starts coming away from the sides.

For the frosting, beat the cream. When it starts to thicken add the sugar and beat until it holds a soft peak. Fold in the cocoa until evenly blended. Cool cake completely before frosting. For the rectangular cake, frost the top and serve squares directly from the pan. For the circular cake, run a knife around the side of the pan and release the springform ring. Use two spatulas to lift the cake from the bottom. Remove the parchment paper from the bottom of the cake. Place the cake on a stand lined with 4 triangles of wax paper placed at the edge of the stand to catch any dripped frosting. Frost the top and sides of the cake and remove the wax paper.

Yield: 12 servings

CHAPTER 5

ADAR

ADAR

With an interesting exception, Jews worldwide celebrate the Festival of Purim on the Fourteenth of Adar. The reason for the date — and the exception — is clear from reading the Book of Esther: "The rest of the Jews in the king's provinces...stood for their lives on the thirteenth of Adar, and on the fourteenth... made it a day of feasting and gladness. But the Jews that were in Shushan assembled together on the thirteenth and on the fourteenth, and...made the fifteenth a day of feasting and gladness. Therefore do the Jews of the villages who dwell in unwalled towns make the fourteenth of Adar a day of gladness and feasting, and a good day of sending food to one another" (The Book of Esther 9:16-19). The Biblical practice continues to this day. To honor the historical importance of what occurred in Shushan, Purim is celebrated on the 15th of Adar in "walled cities", and this day is called "Shushan Purim". Therefore, Jews in New York or New Delhi celebrate Purim on the Fourteenth of Adar — but Jews in Jerusalem's walled Old City wait until the Fifteenth. Thus, a truly dedicated party-goer in Israel could extend the celebration to two days!

The 13th of Adar is marked by observant Jews as the Fast of Esther. Since Esther fasted on that day in contemplation of her meeting with the King and the possible destruction of our people, this day is marked as a minor fast on the Jewish calendar.

There is one more interesting note about the holiday. You may recall that the Jewish calendar has not twelve but thirteen months in seven out of nineteen years. The "extra" month is an "extra" Adar which we call Second Adar. In such years, Purim is celebrated in Second Adar. First Adar, like Cheshvan, has no special holidays or observances besides Shabbat.

PURIM

Adar— the joyous month that ushers in the riotous raucous holiday of Purim! We are urged, "Be Happy, it's Adar!" because this month reminds us of our people's victory over persecution and imminent destruction in ancient Persia. Indeed, Purim actually means lottery, referring to the drawing of chances that would determine on which day the evil Haman would destroy the Jews of Shushan, the capital of Persia.

The Book of Esther, one of the five Megillot (sacred scrolls) in the Bible, is chanted in the synagogue during Purim. It relates the many twists and turns of the intricate and well-known story. Whether one views the narrative as a farcical comedy pitting the good guys against the bad guys, or as a tragi-comedic paradigm of the Jewish experience in the Diaspora — a good time is most definitely had by all. The dramatic reading of the famous Megillah scroll is interrupted by loud groggers (noisemakers) which drown out Haman's name every time the reader tries to chant it.

In addition to the obligation of hearing the chanting of the Megillah, the Rabbis prescribe several other mitzvot in connection with the holiday. We are all to send gifts of food, *mishloach manot*, to our neighbors. We are all to give money to the poor, *mattanot la'evyoneem*. And, finally, we are all to eat a festive meal, so festive in fact that it is perfectly fine to become so drunk that one does not know whether to bless Mordecai and curse Haman — or just the opposite! Costumes are *de rigeur*, as well as simple or elaborate Purim plays, comedies and musicales, so-called *Purimspiels*.

When we discuss the food of this holiday, there is no question which dish has the leading role — that triangular pastry filled with fruit that we call the *hamantasch* (pl. *hamantaschen*). This word, which means Haman's pocket, may also refer to Haman's three-cornered hat or his pointy ears. In fact, in Israel, they are called "*Oznei Haman*", which means "Haman's ears". When we eat the *hamantasch*, we are consuming, devouring and vanquishing Haman — and it seems that most people take this responsibility very seriously! Other culinary traditions include the use of wine in many Purim dishes, as well as the use of poppy seeds. The latter find their way into cakes and cookies as well as hamantaschen. In fact, some have suggested a relationship between the Yiddish word for poppyseed — *mohn* (pronounced mawn) — and the Yiddish/Hebrew pronunciation of Haman (Hah-MAWN).

ADAR SHENI
(SECOND ADAR)

Seven times in nineteen years, a full month is added to the Jewish calendar in order to keep the Jewish months roughly equivalent to the revolution of the earth around the sun. This thirteenth month is added to Adar. In such leap years we thus have Adar I and Adar II. In such years, Purim — as well as any other observances tied to the Jewish calendar (i.e., anniversary of a Bar/Bat Mitzvah) — are celebrated in Adar II. The leap year obviously pushes all the following months and their holidays about thirty days later relative to the solar year. Therefore, Passover, Shavuot, the High Holidays and Chanukah all seem to come late in relation to the solar calendar.

MENU *for* PURIM

Coq au Vin

•

Steamed Baby New Potatoes

•

Chocolate Mousse

•

Hamantaschen

COQ AU VIN

This chicken in wine recipe is a festive dish which matches the mood of the holiday.

2 roasting chickens, each chicken cut up in eighths
Seasoned salt *(I like the Lawry's® brand which contains paprika and is reddish in color)*
½ cup flour
½ cup seasoned bread crumbs
½ teaspoon dried tarragon leaves
2 tablespoons margarine
4 tablespoons oil
1 large onion, diced
1 ½ cups good red wine
½ cup beef bouillon or chicken broth
1 tablespoon tomato paste
1 teaspoon beef concentrate (or 1 beef-flavored cube)
2 cloves garlic, crushed
1 tablespoon flour
1 (15-ounce) can small carrots or sliced carrots, drained
1 (15-ounce) jar small onions, drained
16 baby new potatoes, steamed for about 15 minutes until tender

Rinse and pat dry chicken pieces. Season chicken with seasoned salt. Place chicken in a glass dish, cover, and chill in the refrigerator overnight. The next day, roll chicken in mixture of flour, bread crumbs and tarragon. Preheat oven to 375 degrees. In a frying pan, brown the chicken pieces in margarine and oil, then transfer pieces to an ovenproof dish. Sprinkle with diced onion. Bake uncovered at 375 degrees for 20 minutes. Lower heat to 325 degrees and bake 20 minutes more. Pour wine over chicken and bake 20 minutes. Mix broth, tomato paste, beef concentrate, garlic and 1 tablespoon flour and pour over chicken. Bake 30 minutes. The chicken will bake uncovered during the entire cooking process. Baste and turn chicken at intervals. Add carrots and onions 15 minutes before removing chicken from oven. Serve with steamed baby new potatoes.

Yield: 8 servings

CHOCOLATE MOUSSE

5 tablespoons boiling water
6 ounces semi-sweet chocolate chips
4 eggs, separated
2 tablespoons cognac
1 teaspoon instant coffee (I prefer decaffeinated crystals.)
½ teaspoon vanilla extract
½ teaspoon almond extract
½ pint non-dairy whipping cream or heavy cream

Place hot water in blender. Add chips. Beat on high for six seconds, scraping sides of blender. Add egg yolks, cognac, coffee, vanilla and almond extract. Blend five seconds on high. Add egg whites. Blend on low speed one minute.

Scrape chocolate mixture into a mixing bowl and allow to cool to room temperature. Whip cream, then fold into chocolate mixture. Pour mousse into individual glasses and chill thoroughly for a few hours or overnight.

Yield: 6 to 8 servings

N O T E : *If one prefers not to use fresh egg whites, the dried egg whites available in the baking section of the grocery are a fine substitution. Take 2 tablespoons plus 2 teaspoons of dried egg whites and reconstitute with ½ cup warm water. Stir for 2 minutes until powder is completely dissolved. This mixture is equivalent to 4 egg whites and may then be added to the blender instead of the fresh egg whites.*

HAMANTASCHEN

COOKIE DOUGH:
1 ⅓ cups unsalted margarine or unsalted butter (room temperature)
1 cup sugar
2 eggs
4 cups flour
4 teaspoons baking powder
2 teaspoons salt
6 tablespoons ice water or milk
2 teaspoons vanilla extract

Cream margarine (or butter) and sugar together. Add eggs, one at a time, until well blended. Sift flour, baking powder, and salt together. Using a fork, add dry ingredients alternately with liquid (water or milk) and vanilla to form a ball. Knead the dough lightly in the bowl. Chill at least two hours after wrapping well in plastic wrap dusted with flour. Divide dough in quarters. Refrigerate remaining dough until ready to roll. On lightly floured surface, roll dough to ¼-inch thickness. Cut into three-inch circles. Place approximately one teaspoon filling on each circle. Form into triangles. Place on cookie sheets. Bake at 375 degrees for 12 to 15 minutes. Place cookies on rack to cool.

FILLING:
In a saucepan, combine:
1 ½ cups golden raisins
⅔ cup of pitted dried prunes, cut up
6 tablespoons poppy seeds
6 tablespoons honey
Pinch salt
1 ½ teaspoons of grated lemon rind
2 tablespoons water

Heat gently on low heat until soft and well-combined. Let cool. Place in food processor and process with steel blade to form a moist filling.

Yield: About 4 dozen cookies

NOTE: *A variety of excellent ready-made fillings is available in the Baker Brand®
from the Solo Company.*

POPPY SEED RING COOKIES

Poppy seeds (or mohn in Yiddish) are a common ingredient in many Eastern European pastries. A Midrash or legend has it that Queen Esther subsisted on poppy seeds and chick peas in order to keep kosher while living in the palace in Shushan. This story may be one reason that poppy seeds figure prominently in recipes for Purim (see illustration on page 181).

(see illustration on page 181)

DOUGH:
2 ½ cups flour
1 teaspoon baking powder
¼ teaspoon salt
½ cup sugar
1 cup (2 sticks) unsalted butter, cut into pats
½ cup (4 ounces) sour cream
3 tablespoons poppy seeds
1 egg yolk, lightly beaten (reserve egg white for topping)
1 teaspoon vanilla extract

TOPPING:
1 egg white, beaten until foamy
½ cup granulated sugar or sanding sugar (a large crystal, decorative sugar available online or in gourmet culinary shops)

Preheat oven to 350 degrees. Line two cookie sheets with parchment paper.

Place flour, baking powder, salt and sugar in a large mixing bowl and blend with a fork. Add the butter and sour cream to the flour mixture. Use a pastry blender or two knives to cut the wet ingredients into the dry ingredients until dough has the consistency of small peas. Add the poppy seeds and blend well. Add the beaten egg yolk and vanilla, and gather the dough together with a fork until it forms a ball. Lightly knead the dough in the bowl to complete the blending process. Place the dough on a piece of lightly floured wax paper and cut it into four parts. Flatten each part into a circular disc and wrap in lightly floured plastic wrap. Chill thoroughly for several hours.

After chilling, remove the dough from the fridge and work with one part at a time. Take about 2 teaspoons of dough and roll it between your fingers to form a "snake" about four inches long. Bend the dough into a circle and seal the edges to form a ring.

Set up two small bowls for completing the topping, one bowl containing the beaten egg white, and one the sugar. Dip the top of the cookie first in the egg white, then in the sugar. Place on prepared cookie sheets. Bake at 350 degrees for 20 minutes.

Yield: About 64 cookies

ADAR

CHAPTER 6

NISAN

NISAN

DATES *of* THE JEWISH HOLIDAYS IN NISAN

Although the first day of the seventh month (Tishri) is the popular New Year (Rosh Hashanah), Nisan is the first legal month of the Jewish calendar because it was the month of the Exodus and the month from which the commencement of a king's reign was reckoned. In Biblical days, this month was called "Aviv", the springtime month: "You shall eat unleavened bread seven days, as I commanded you, in the time appointed in the month of Aviv" (Exodus 23:15). In later times the name of this month became Nisan. The Babylonian word Nisan refers to "flight", and there could not be a more appropriate title for this month. It is after all the time in which the Jewish people fled from slavery to freedom and became a nation.

We mark the period of time (49 days or 7 weeks) between Passover and Shavuot with a custom called "The counting of the Omer", which commemorates the period between the start of the Exodus (Passover), and the giving of the Torah on Mount Sinai (Shavuot). The "Omer" was simply a "measure"—in this case a measure of barley, which was brought to the Temple each day for 49 days, starting on the second day of Passover. In the Temple, the Priests burned some of this grain as an offering to God. After forty-nine days of counting the Omer, we reach the fiftieth day, the holiday of Shavuot. This counting thus links the holidays of Passover and Shavuot. On Passover, we declared our freedom. On Shavuot, we received our Torah.

The period of the Omer in the traditional community is a somber one because of events that took place during the Roman occupation. Observant Jews do not conduct weddings and some do not even shave. These prohibitions are lifted on the 33rd Day of the Counting (Lag Ba'omer, the 18th of Iyyar) and, in some communities, on Israel Independence Day, the 5th of Iyyar.

There is one even sadder observance which occurs on the 27th day of Nisan. It was during this time in 1943 that the Jews in the Warsaw Ghetto rebelled against their Nazi oppressors. Since 1951, the 27th of Nisan has been observed as the Jewish commemoration of the tragedy of the Holocaust.

15 NISAN:

FIRST DAY OF PASSOVER

(First Seder occurs the night before)

•

16 NISAN:

SECOND DAY OF PASSOVER

In traditional communities, the Second Day of Passover (with the Second Seder occurring the night before). On this night, we begin Counting the Omer.

•

22 NISAN:

SEVENTH DAY OF PASSOVER

•

23 NISAN:

EIGHTH DAY OF PASSOVER

(not observed by Reform Jews or by Jews in Israel)

•

27 NISAN:

YOM HASHO'AH V'HAG'VURAH

(Full English translation: "Day of Devastation and Heroism" — but most refer to it simply as "Yom Hashoah", Holocaust Remembrance Day)

PASSOVER

Passover is an awe-inspiring holiday infused by the majesty of the biblical story of the Exodus from Egypt and the beauty of the traditional Seder service and meal. As the holiday approaches, the pace quickens. Families complete the thorough house cleaning, bringing out Passover housewares and preparing for the Seder. When I was a child, my father would take us to the Lower East Side where he grew up (I called it "the little old-fashioned village") to purchase matzah and Passover wine. We visited the matzah factory and watched the making of the unleavened bread. Then we went to Schapiro's wine shop where we could taste samples right from the barrels. Their ad wasn't just words — it seemed so thick and sweet that you really could "cut it with a knife." Finally we got our large horseradish root which would be peeled and grated and transformed into the unforgettable bitter herbs.

On Passover night, we drove to Brooklyn for Seder at my Aunt Sarah and Uncle Ira's house. The table was so beautiful, set with silver and cobalt blue china and a crystallized grape centerpiece. We sipped the traditional four cups of wine from tiny thimble-like silver cups. Even as children, we were allowed to have as much as we wanted and, as a result, I always ended up fast asleep on the living room couch!

The Seder is a beautiful religious service which takes place at home on the evening before the fifteenth of Nisan. We read and sing from a book called the Haggadah which contains the story of the holiday, as well as rabbinic commentaries, legends, assorted narratives and wonderful songs. Everyone actively participates in the readings "as if we ourselves had been saved from Egypt." The text reminds us that we were strangers in a foreign land, thus teaching us that we must never be insensitive to others. We left Egypt in great haste, and we were not able to let our bread rise in the customary manner. So we ate flat unleavened bread which we commemorate by eating matzah that entire week.

Matzah is but one of many symbols associated with Passover. The Seder plate at the center of the table has many more, each a cue to the dramatic story. The bitter herbs (*maror*) remind us of the bitterness of our lives in bondage. The lamb shank (*pesach*) represents our rescue from the Angel of Death when it "passed over" our homes. The roasted egg (*beytza*) stands for rebirth, the cycle of life ever going around, winter always giving way to spring. The green parsley (*karpas*) is springtime itself — but, by dipping it into salt water, we remember that it is not spring for everyone. Our ancestors shed tears; so do many human beings in our own day. Finally, the mixture of apples, nuts and wine called *charoset* represents the bricks we were forced to make when we were slaves.

With the lighting of the candles and the chanting of the blessing over wine *(Kiddush)*, the beautiful ritual unfolds. Once more we recall the powerful story of enslavement and freedom. Once more history comes alive as we participate in the Passover Seder.

ON YOUR SEDER TABLE, YOU SHOULD HAVE:
1. a small dish of salt water for dipping parsley
2. a pitcher of water and a large bowl for hand washing
3. a plate with three pieces of matzah, one above the other
4. a wine cup filled to the brim (Elijah's cup)
5. the Seder Plate

ON YOUR SEDER PLATE, YOU SHOULD HAVE:
1. a shank bone *(pesach)*
2. a roasted egg *(beytza)*
3. parsley *(karpas)*
4. horseradish *(maror)*
5. *charoset*
6. The use of lettuce, celery or endive as a second bitter herb *(chazeret)* is optional.

MENU *for* PASSOVER

Gelfite Fish and Horseradish

•

Chicken Soup with herb/carrot garnish *(page 10)*

•

Matzah Balls (Kneidlach) *(Pages 11 and 12)*

•

Citrus Chicken

•

Potato Kugel

•

Asparagus with chopped cashews

•

Gloria's Heimish Fruit Compote

•

Passover Chocolate Chip Cake

•

Strawberries

•

Non-dairy whipped topping

•

Crystallized Grapes

FIERY GRATED HORSERADISH

Because of the strong, unpleasant fumes given off by the grated horseradish root, I always avoided the kitchen when my Dad made his horseradish for Passover. How I wish I had been less skittish — I would have had his recipe! This one comes from my dear friend Elaine in Louisville, who makes a beautiful Seder for many guests every year.

1 pound horseradish root
⅔ cup white vinegar
⅓ cup of juice from canned beets

Rinse and peel horseradish root. Cut it into pieces that will fit into the feeder tube of the food processor. Because the root is so hard, process it in two stages. First, use the grating disc to give a coarse, grated consistency. Then transfer the grated root to a mixing bowl and replace the grating disc with the steel blade. Add the grated horseradish back into the processor bowl and chop to a fine consistency. Finally, combine the chopped root with vinegar and beet juice in a mixing bowl. Store in a glass jar in the refrigerator.

Yield: 2 cups of fiery horseradish

NOTE: *The fumes given off by the grated root are very strong, and can cause the eyes to sting. Be sure to work in a well-ventilated kitchen. If the eyes start to sting, back off for a moment and use a cold compress. One can also wear goggles to protect the eyes.*

CHAROSET

3 large apples, peeled, cored and cut into chunks
1 cup walnut pieces
⅓ cup sweet Passover wine
1 teaspoon ground cinnamon
1 tablespoon honey

Place apples and nuts in food processor and pulse until ingredients are coarsely chopped. Add remaining ingredients and pulse just a few more seconds to blend. Maintain coarse texture.

Yield: About 4 cups

NOTE: *This recipe may be made the day before.*

NISAN

CITRUS CHICKEN

This recipe is best when the chicken is marinated overnight.

2 (3-3 ½) pound chickens, cut in eighths
2 teaspoons kosher salt

MARINADE:
2 garlic cloves, minced
4 shallots, minced
2 tablespoons fresh ginger, minced
4 tablespoons vegetable oil
½ cup white wine

COATING FOR CHICKEN:
6 ounces of premium quality orange or tangerine jam or fruit spread
   (Avoid any jam that contains corn syrup, as the corn ingredient is not kosher for
   Passover.)
1 tablespoon fresh rosemary, chopped fine
1 tablespoon fresh thyme leaves
½ cup water to add to the roasting pan

The day before rinse and dry chicken pieces. Sprinkle each chicken piece with salt.
Combine marinade ingredients in a glass bowl. Pour marinade over chicken and
marinate in the refrigerator overnight. The next day spread each chicken piece
on both sides with the jam and sprinkle with rosemary and thyme. Place chicken
pieces skin side up on a shallow roasting pan. Add remaining marinade and water
to roasting pan. Bake uncovered at 350 degrees for 1 ½ hours.

Yield: 8 servings

POTATO KUGEL

8 medium russet potatoes
2 large onions
5 large eggs, beaten with a whisk
1 teaspoon salt
⅓ cup oil
¾ cup matzah meal

Preheat oven to 425 degrees. Spray a 13 x 9 x 2-inch baking dish with vegetable spray.

Peel potatoes and onions, and cut into pieces that will fit into the tube of the food processor. With the shredding disc of the processor, grate the potatoes and onions. Place potato mixture in a large bowl.

In a small bowl whisk eggs, oil and salt together. Add this mixture to potatoes and blend. Sprinkle potato mixture with matzah meal and blend well. Spoon potato mixture into the greased baking dish.

Bake uncovered at 425 degrees for 15 minutes. Then turn down the temperature to 350 degrees and bake for 30 minutes more.

Yield: 12 to 14 servings

ASPARAGUS
WITH CHOPPED CASHEWS

3 pounds asparagus
3 tablespoons non-dairy margarine
½ cup unsalted chopped cashews
¼ teaspoon salt

Snap ends off asparagus spears and rinse well in a large bowl of water. Using a vegetable peeler, remove outer layer from lower end of each asparagus spear. Lay tough ends in a large pot with two inches of water. These ends will form a scaffolding for steaming the delicate asparagus, and will be discarded when the cooking is completed. Lay trimmed asparagus on top of the tough ends. Cover pot and bring water to the boil. Steam for 4 to 5 minutes, being careful not to overcook. With tongs, remove spears from the pot, drain off water, and place asparagus on the serving dish. Discard the tough ends. Melt margarine and add cashews and salt to the melted margarine. Pour margarine mixture over asparagus and serve.

Yield: 12 servings

N O T E : *Using the tough ends as a support for the tender asparagus spears during the steaming process prevents the spears from becoming overcooked and soggy.*

GLORIA'S HEIMISH FRUIT COMPOTE

The word "heimish" implies a homey or down to earth quality, which in fact describes Gloria very well. This compote makes a delicious accompaniment to meat or chicken at the Seder meal. It should be made the day before so that the flavors can meld.

3 cups dried pitted prunes
1 cup dried apples
1 cup dried apricots
1 cup dried peaches or pears
½ cup golden raisins
Grated rind of 1 lemon
Juice of ½ lemon
2 tablespoons brown sugar
2 cups water
1 cup sweet Passover Concord grape wine

Cut fruit into small pieces and place in a 4-quart pot. Add lemon rind, lemon juice, brown sugar, water and wine. Bring up to the simmer and cook, covered, for about 30 minutes. Cool mixture and refrigerate overnight. Serve at the Seder meal as a side dish.

Yield: 8 cups of compote

BOBBIE'S PASSOVER SPONGE CAKE

Passover sponge cakes have no leavening ingredients, and depend on eggs alone for their airy consistency. Therefore they can collapse after they are baked during the cooling process. The tube pans, with the three "feet" attached to the rim, allow you to cool the cake in an upside down position to prevent it from sinking. Some cookbooks tell you to invert the cake by placing the tube over a bottle. I have had difficulty finding a bottle with a neck thin enough to fit the opening of the tube. Therefore I would recommend the pan with the "feet". In addition, in this recipe the pan is not greased; this allows the cake to "climb" up the sides of the pan while it bakes. This recipe comes from my friend Bobbie. When I tasted it at a Sisterhood Choir luncheon, I knew it was a winner.

½ cup matzah cake meal
⅓ cup potato starch
8 large eggs, separated
2 additional large eggs, not separated
1 ½ cups sugar
¼ cup fresh lemon juice
½ teaspoon cinnamon
1 tablespoon sugar for topping

Preheat the oven to 350 degrees. Use a 10-inch tube pan (4 inches deep) with a removable bottom and "feet". Cut a piece of parchment paper to fit the bottom of the pan. Do not grease the pan.

Sift cake meal and potato starch together three times and set aside. Whip 8 egg whites until stiff peaks form, then set aside. In another mixing bowl beat egg yolks and two additional whole eggs. Slowly add sugar and beat for several minutes on medium speed until mixture is light yellow. Beat in lemon juice on low speed. Add dry ingredients to egg mixture on low speed until just blended (do not overbeat). Fold in beaten egg whites by hand. Pour one half of the batter into the prepared pan. Sprinkle with ¼ teaspoon cinnamon. Pour in the remaining batter.

Sprinkle the top with ¼ teaspoon cinnamon mixed with 1 tablespoon of sugar. Bake for 45 minutes at 350 degrees. Turn the cake upside down on a rack to cool. When completely cooled, run a knife around the sides of the pan. Lift up the cake by the tube. Using two spatulas, lift it off the bottom. Peel off the parchment and place cake on a serving plate.

Yield: 12 servings

NISAN

PASSOVER CHOCOLATE CHIP CAKE

This recipe comes from my college roommate's mother Mae, who graciously shared it with me when I visited their Philadelphia home many years ago during spring break, which coincided with Passover. It has been a favorite ever since.

1 large tube or Bundt pan
Vegetable cooking spray
8 eggs, separated
1 cup sugar
¼ cup honey
Grated rind of one orange
¼ cup orange juice
½ cup Concord grape wine
1 cup matzah meal, sifted
2 teaspoons cinnamon
Dash of salt
⅓ cup chocolate chips
¾ cup chopped walnuts

Preheat oven to 350 degrees. Spray a large tube pan or Bundt pan with vegetable cooking spray.

Beat egg whites until stiff. Set aside. Cream yolks and sugar. Add honey, rind, orange juice and wine. Add matzah meal, cinnamon and salt. Fold in beaten egg whites. Fold in chocolate chips and nuts. Bake for 45 minutes at 350 degrees.

Yield: 10 to 12 servings

CRYSTALLIZED GRAPES

As a child I was fascinated by the frosted appearance of the crystallized grapes on my Aunt Sarah's Seder table centerpiece. They are delicious to eat and can be used in small bunches to garnish other desserts. For a centerpiece, large grapes are more effective. For a dessert garnish, the smaller grapes look better.

1 bunch of very fresh and firm green grapes
1 bunch of very fresh and firm purple grapes
2 egg whites
1 teaspoon water
Granulated sugar

The day before you are planning to make this recipe, wash grapes and lay them out overnight on paper towels so they are completely dry by the next day. Then, on the following day, cut the grapes into small bunches of about 6 grapes each. Beat egg whites with water until slightly foamy. With a soft pastry brush, paint grapes with egg white mixture and sprinkle generously with sugar until they take on a frosted appearance. Place grape bunches on parchment or wax paper to dry thoroughly for at least several hours. When the grapes are dry, arrange bunches by themselves or with other fruits to make an attractive centerpiece. Small bunches may also be used as a dessert garnish.

N O T E : *I have not had a problem using fresh egg whites. For those who prefer not to use raw egg whites, there is a dried egg white product available in the baking aisle of the grocery. To obtain the equivalent of two egg whites, add ¼ cup warm water to 4 level teaspoons of dried egg whites and stir for 2 minutes until the powdered egg whites are dissolved. Then proceed as you would with the fresh egg whites.*

CHAPTER 7

IYYAR

IYYAR

DATES *of* THE JEWISH HOLIDAYS IN IYYAR

4 IYYAR:
YOM HAZIKKARON
NATIONAL DAY OF REMEMBRANCE

5 IYYAR:
YOM HA'ATZMA'UT
ISRAEL INDEPENDENCE DAY

18 IYYAR:
LAG BA'OMER
33RD DAY OF THE OMER

28 IYYAR:
YOM YERUSHALAYIM
JERUSALEM DAY

IYYAR

Both Iyyar and Israel begin with the letter "I", an excellent way to associate the many Israel-based holidays that occur during this month. The name of the month has the connotation of "light" or "blossom" in Babylonian, and it was called "Ziv" ("brightness") in the Bible. Yet this month occurs during the Omer, the solemn period between Passover and Shavuot during which marriages are prohibited and observant Jews do not shave.

So this month is both somber and joyful. The generally serious atmosphere of the Omer period is broken by several important and joyful dates, all revolving around an aspect of the history of Israel. The most dramatic of these is the fifth day of the month, on which Israel's independence was proclaimed in 1948. The day before this, 4 Iyyar, is observed in Israel as Yom Hazikkaron, National Day of Remembrance, on which we remember the soldiers who fell fighting for that independence, and those who lost their lives in the many subsequent battles that have occurred since the creation of the State of Israel.

In our tradition, we remember a plague that destroyed many students of the great Rabbi Akiba, perhaps around 130 C.E. On 18 Iyyar, the thirty-third day of the Omer, the plague ceased. Accordingly, the prohibitions associated with the Omer are lifted. Weddings may be solemnized, and the joyful day is marked by outdoor games, archery contests, cookouts, campouts, bonfires and the like.

Finally, on 28 Iyyar, we remember that date in 1967 when Jerusalem was reunited during the Six Day War (June 7 on the secular calendar).

COOKOUT MENU *for* LAG BA'OMER

Gazpacho

•

Grilled Hamburgers and Hot Dogs with Buns

•

Ketchup, Mustard, Sweet Relish,
and Sauerkraut to garnish Grilled Meat

•

Cole Slaw

•

Roasted Potato Wedges with Onions

•

Strawberry Rhubarb Pie

GAZPACHO

BROTH:
3 tablespoons olive oil
1 tablespoon fresh lemon juice
1 tablespoon red wine vinegar
1 teaspoon Worcestershire sauce
¼ teaspoon salt
⅛ teaspoon garlic powder
6 cups tomato juice

VEGETABLES:
2 cups seedless English cucumbers, cut in small dice
2 cups seeded tomatoes, in small dice
⅓ cup carrots, in small dice
½ cup celery, strings removed, in small dice
¾ cup sweet red pepper, in small dice
¼ cup green bell pepper, in small dice
½ cup red onion, in small dice (optional)
2 tablespoons chopped parsley
2 tablespoons chopped sweet basil

GARNISH:
½ cup uncooked, fresh corn kernels cut off the cob and tossed with ½ teaspoon sugar
½ cup diced avocado

In a large bowl whisk olive oil, lemon juice, vinegar, Worcestershire sauce, salt and garlic powder. Add tomato juice to bowl and stir. Prepare all the vegetables in uniformly small dice and add to the bowl. Chill for several hours or overnight. Garnish with corn kernels and avocado and serve chilled.

Yield: 12 to 14 servings

GRILLED HAMBURGERS

2 pounds ground beef
2 tablespoons ketchup
1 tablespoon Worcestershire sauce
      (See page 201, number 7 on the dietary laws.)
1 teaspoon Dijon mustard

Combine all ingredients and blend well. Divide mixture into 8 parts and form patties. Grill about 4-5 minutes on each side for medium doneness. For best results, flip burgers only one time.

Yield: 8 servings

COLE SLAW

2 tablespoons sugar
1 shot glass (2 ounces) white vinegar
⅛ teaspoon celery seeds
¾ cup mayonnaise
½ teaspoon salt
Half a large head of cabbage or a 1 pound bag shredded cabbage
1 small onion, grated (optional)
1 large carrot
3 radishes

Add the first 5 ingredients to the bottom of a large bowl and mix well.

Cut cabbage into pieces to fit into the food processor. Discard the core. Process the cabbage, carrot and radishes with the thin slaw slicing blade. Add sliced vegetables and onion to the bowl with the dressing and toss well. Chill for several hours or overnight to allow the flavors to blend.

Yield: 12 servings

N O T E : *If serving this recipe for a dairy meal, one may substitute ½ cup mayonnaise and ½ cup low fat sour cream for the ¾ cup mayonnaise. This substitution will result in a lighter consistency.*

ROASTED POTATO WEDGES
WITH ONIONS

Vegetable cooking spray
4 tablespoons vegetable oil
1 teaspoon garlic salt
½ teaspoon sweet paprika
6 medium russet potatoes
1 large onion, peeled and diced

Preheat oven to 375 degrees.

Spray a roasting pan with cooking spray. Place oil, garlic salt and paprika in the pan and blend. Scrub potatoes well. Slice each potato in half, and then each half into 4 pieces to give 8 wedges. Repeat the process with all of the potatoes. Place potato wedges and diced onion in the roasting pan and toss with the oil mixture to coat all pieces. Bake at 375 degrees for about an hour, turning pieces every 15 minutes for even browning to achieve a nice crust.

Yield: 8 to 10 servings

STRAWBERRY RHUBARB PIE

DOUBLE CRUST RECIPE FOR A 9-INCH PIE PLATE:
2 cups flour
1 teaspoon salt
½ cup chilled solid vegetable shortening, cut into ½-inch cubes
¼ cup chilled parve margarine (or butter), cut into ½-inch cubes
6-8 tablespoons ice water

FILLING:
4 cups fresh rhubarb, cut into ¾-inch pieces
2 cups sliced fresh strawberries
1 cup plus 2 tablespoons sugar
2 tablespoons cornstarch
⅛ teaspoon salt
2 large eggs

FOR EGG GLAZE AND CINNAMON SUGAR
TO FINISH THE TOP CRUST:
1 egg yolk beaten with 1 teaspoon water
1 tablespoon sugar mixed with ¼ teaspoon cinnamon for dusting the top crust

Preheat the oven to 425 degrees. Use a 9-inch pie plate.

FOR THE CRUST:
Place flour and salt in a mixing bowl. Cut shortening and margarine (or shortening and butter) into the flour mixture with a pastry blender until it has the consistency of small peas. Add ice water, one tablespoon at a time, using a fork to gather the dough into a ball. Add only enough water so that dough holds together. Briefly knead the dough into a ball. Cut it into two pieces so that one piece is slightly bigger. This bigger piece will be for the bottom crust. Wrap each ball in plastic wrap and chill dough at least 30 minutes. Place the larger piece of dough on a floured board. Flour a rolling pin and the board as needed and roll the dough into a circle about 11 inches in diameter. Roll the crust over the rolling pin and unroll it over the pie plate. Take the second ball of dough and roll it out in a similar manner to a diameter of about 10 inches.

FOR THE FILLING:

In a bowl combine the rhubarb and strawberries with the sugar. In another bowl beat the eggs, salt and cornstarch together and pour over the fruit mixture. Blend thoroughly. Place the filling in the pie shell. Brush the egg glaze on the outer edge of the bottom pie shell. Roll the top crust over the rolling pin and place it over the filling. With the rolling pin, press down on the edges of the top and bottom crust to seal them together. Trim off uneven pieces of dough, leaving enough of an edge for crimping. Use a fork or your thumb and third finger to crimp the dough into an attractive edge. Brush the top of the crust with the egg glaze and dust lightly with the cinnamon sugar. Make several slits in the top crust so that steam can escape during the baking process.

Bake at 425 degrees for 15 minutes. Then turn temperature down to 350 degrees and bake 30 minutes more. When baking is complete, place pie on a wire rack for cooling.

Yield: 8 servings

CHAPTER 8

SIVAN

SIVAN

DATES *of* THE JEWISH HOLIDAYS IN SIVAN

6 SIVAN:
SHAVUOT

7 SIVAN:
**SECOND DAY OF SHAVUOT IN
TRADITIONAL COMMUNITIES OUTSIDE
ISRAEL**

SHAVUOT

Shavuot — the best kept secret in Jewish life.

Besides Shabbat, the Jewish holidays are categorized into three groups: High Holidays (Rosh Hashanah and Yom Kippur); Festivals (Passover, Shavuot and Sukkot); and Minor Holidays (Chanukah, Tu B'Shevat, Purim and others). The High Holidays and the Festivals have their roots in Torah and in our ancient history as an agricultural people. These five observances are marked by precise sacrifices prescribed in the Torah, and work is prohibited on all five.

The minor holidays were added to our calendar after the content of the Torah was finalized. They came about in response to quasi-historical narratives. Purim is based on a fantastic melodrama that is included in the Bible but not in the Torah. The story of Chanukah is not even in the Bible. Lag Ba'omer, Tu B'Shevat — these observances, like Israel Independence Day or Yom Ha'shoah, evolved in response to historical circumstances long after the Bible was codified. Work and daily life continue uninterrupted on these holidays.

Yet there is little question that the "minor" holidays, particularly Chanukah, have captured the hearts and the imagination of our people far more than the statutory Festival called Shavuot. One of the most beautiful of our observances, Shavuot celebrates the harvesting of the first fruits, as well as the receiving of the Ten Commandments. Seven weeks and a day separate Passover from Shavuot, the exact interval between the Exodus and the Revelation at Sinai.

Dairy foods are traditionally served on Shavuot. Various explanations for this custom have been offered including the abundance of lush grazing land at this time of the year resulting in milk and milk products. Mention is also made of the "whiteness" of dairy reminding us of the purity of the Torah, which was given to us on the way to the "Land of Milk and Honey".

A BRUNCH *for* SHAVUOT

This menu would also work well for a baby naming or Bris.

Cheese Blintzes with Sour Cream and Blueberry Topping

•

Cold Poached Salmon with Cucumber Dill Sauce

•

Endive, Grapefruit and Avocado Salad

•

New York Style Cheesecake

•

Rugelach

•

Seasonal Fresh Fruit such as Sliced Melon
and Whole Strawberries

SIVAN

TRADITIONAL CHEESE BLINTZES WITH A FRENCH FLAIR

My recipe collection is like a patchwork of the various places where I have lived and the two careers that I have enjoyed. Before training as a physician, I taught French to middle school and high school students, including a terrific group of ninth graders in Bethany, Connecticut. We created a French dinner, and this crêpe recipe was donated by two students in the class, Jack and Derrick.

Grease an 8-inch crêpe pan with butter.

THE BATTER: SIFT TOGETHER
¾ cup flour
¼ teaspoon salt
¼ teaspoon baking powder
1 teaspoon sugar

BLEND WITH:
3 eggs
2 tablespoons melted butter
1 ⅓ cups milk

Whisk batter ingredients together until smooth. Allow batter to rest for 30 minutes. Heat a well-seasoned 8-inch crêpe pan which has been lightly greased with butter. Pour about a ¼ cup batter and rotate the pan to cover the bottom. Fry over medium high heat until golden spots begin to form on the underside and the edges begin to come away from the sides. Use a spatula to lift the edge of the crêpe and flip to cook a few more seconds on the other side. Immediately remove crêpe to a plate. Grease the pan lightly as needed during the frying process. If you have a heavy pan, one or two greasings may be all that are needed. Eventually, you will become more skillful at producing thin pancakes, and you will be able to use less batter. The crêpes have an elastic quality and are easy to flip. They may be piled on top of one another until ready to fill.

THE FILLING:
1 pound Farmer cheese (a dry type of cottage cheese)
2 large eggs
1 ½ tablespoons sugar
Combine all ingredients and mix well

TO ASSEMBLE BLINTZES:
Spoon 2-3 tablespoons filling lengthwise in center of crepe. Fold two sides over filling. Then roll blintz to make a secure rectangular package.

TO COMPLETE BLINTZES:
2 tablespoons butter
8 ounces sour cream
1 can cherry or blueberry pie filling

Melt 2 tablespoons butter in frying pan. Place blintzes seam-side down and fry until golden. Flip and repeat process on reverse side. Serve with sour cream and cherry or blueberry pie filling.

Yield: 5 to 6 servings

EGG BLINTZ CASSEROLE

If one does not have time to makes blintzes from scratch, this recipe is a quick and easy alternative.

Vegetable cooking spray
½ stick butter or margarine
10 frozen cheese blintzes (do not thaw)

Spray 13 x 9 x 2-inch oven-proof glass dish with vegetable cooking spray. Melt butter and add to dish. Then place frozen blintzes in a single layer, seam-side down.

7 eggs beaten
½ pint sour cream
¼ cup orange juice
2 teaspoons vanilla extract
2 tablespoons sugar
½ teaspoon salt

Preheat oven to 350 degrees. Beat above 6 ingredients and pour over blintzes. Bake uncovered at 350 degrees for one hour.

Yield: 8 servings

COLD POACHED SALMON WITH CUCUMBER DILL SAUCE

A whole "side" or filet of salmon (which is one half of the fish) is used for this recipe. Using a fish poacher (available online) makes handling the filet easy after it is poached. The fish is poached in a court bouillon, a broth which is "short or brief", meaning that it does not take a long time to prepare. For this recipe the broth takes only 15 minutes to cook before the salmon is added to it. I use a 20-inch long fish poacher for this recipe.

1 3-pound filet or side of salmon

COURT BOUILLON:
2 quarts water
2 cups dry white wine
2 celery stalks, chopped
1 carrot, chopped
3 sprigs parsley
1 lemon peel strip
1 clove garlic
1 medium onion, chopped
2 whole cloves
1 tablespoon kosher salt
1 bay leaf

CUCUMBER DILL SAUCE:
1 cup sour cream
1 cup mayonnaise
1 tablespoon fresh lemon juice
1 cup seeded cucumber, cut in small dice
4 tablespoons fresh chopped dill
½ teaspoon salt

GARNISH:
lemon slices
cucumber slices
grape tomatoes
red onion, sliced

Put salmon aside while the court bouillon is prepared. Place all the other ingredients in the poacher. Place poacher over two burners. Bring ingredients to the boil, then reduce heat, cover and simmer the bouillon for 15 minutes. Place the salmon on the poaching rack, skin side down, and gently lower the filet into the court bouillon. The fish must be completely submerged in the broth. Let bouillon come back to a simmer and poach, covered for 15 minutes. Do not allow the broth to come to a rolling boil, as that may cause the fish to be tough and flaky. Then immediately lift the fish out of the broth with the poaching rack and allow to drain well. Place salmon on the serving plate. Discard broth and vegetables. Garnish with lemon slices, cucumber slices, grape tomatoes and red onion. Serve chilled or at room temperature with cucumber dill sauce.

Blend sauce ingredients. Chill and serve with poached salmon.

Yield: 14 to 16 buffet size servings

ENDIVE, GRAPEFRUIT AND ORANGE SALAD WITH A GINGER LEMON DRESSING

During my fellowship year at the University of Iowa I was fortunate enough to take classes at the Chez Mimi Cooking School with Mimi Gormezano. This delightful light salad comes from her repertoire.

4 small Belgian endives, cut lengthwise into quarters
12 grapefruit sections
12 orange sections
12 avocado slices (optional)

DRESSING:
2 tablespoons maple syrup
3 tablespoons fresh lemon juice
½ teaspoon salt
½ teaspoon freshly grated ginger root

GARNISH:
1 teaspoon lightly toasted sesame seeds

Alternately place slices of endive and sections of the citrus fruit on a platter. If using avocado, alternate avocado slices with endive and citrus. Pour the dressing over the salad. Sprinkle with toasted sesame seeds. Watercress may also be used for a touch of green for those who do not like avocado.

Yield: 4 to 6 servings

MY VERSION OF
KAYSEY'S RICE PUDDING

Kaysey's was a wonderful New York style restaurant near the Shubert Theater in New Haven, Connecticut. Because of its proximity to the Shubert, which showcased so many pre-Broadway productions, it attracted a stellar theater crowd. It was there that a young theater buff like my husband had the opportunity to meet such Broadway luminaries as Tennessee Williams, Richard Rodgers and Mike Nichols during pre-Broadway tryouts. Kaysey's rice pudding dessert was a favorite of mine and my mother-in-law Ethel. It arrived chilled in a dessert dish piled high with whipped cream. When I requested the recipe, I was told that one had only to combine rice, milk and sugar and cook it in a pot for about 40 minutes until creamy. Therefore my version is pretty simple — no eggs or cream are added. I do add vanilla, and one may add raisins or chopped apples for contrast. After scalding the milk on the stove, I combine it with the other ingredients and finish the cooking in the oven.

Preheat oven to 350 degrees. Grease a 1 ½-quart baking dish with butter.
(A soufflé dish works well.)

1 tablespoon softened butter for greasing the baking dish
1 quart whole milk
½ cup uncooked long grain rice
¼ cup sugar
½ teaspoon vanilla extract
¼ cup golden raisins or diced apple
Whipped cream for topping
Cinnamon to sprinkle on top

Scald the milk in a heavy-bottomed saucepan until steam begins to rise from the surface. Watch carefully or the milk will boil over before you know it, making a terrible mess. Turn off the heat and add uncooked rice, sugar, vanilla and stir. Pour this mixture into a greased 1 ½-quart ovenproof baking dish or soufflé dish. Bake the pudding uncovered at 350 degrees for about 45 minutes until creamy. During the cooking process, stir every 15 minutes. Add the raisins or apples during the last 20 minutes of cooking. Serve warm or cold with whipped cream and a sprinkling of cinnamon. The pudding will continue to thicken as it cools.

Yield: 6 servings

NEW YORK STYLE CHEESECAKE

This cake is a lighter, home style version of the famous Lindy's cheesecake. Lindy's Broadway restaurant was a favorite hangout for entertainers, tourists and mobsters alike from the 1920's until the late 1960's. Milton Berle, the famous comedian, was a frequent patron, and one evening I actually saw him holding court at a large rectangular table near the front door. Lindy's cheesecake is legendary. Each slice was large, expensive and completely worth the money and the calories.

Cheesecakes are easy to make as long as certain rules are observed. Even though the mixing of the cake does not take much time, planning ahead is essential.

1. Use a springform pan which makes unmolding easy. Since the cheesecake will bake in a water bath and the springform pan is not watertight, wrap the bottom of the pan in heavy duty foil that goes about two thirds of the way up the side of the pan. If a few drops of water should leak in, that's perfectly fine. A small amount of water will not affect the cake.

2. The cream cheese, eggs and butter should be at room temperature.

3. Be sure to scrape down the sides and bottom of the bowl after beating the cream cheese, and after each addition of another ingredient, in order to eliminate any lumps.

4. Beat at medium speed to avoid incorporating too much air into the batter. This will maintain a creamy consistency.

5. After baking time is complete, turn off the oven and leave the oven door ajar. Let the cake sit in the oven in the water bath for one hour before removing from the oven and placing it on a cooling rack. The gradual cooldown will prevent cracking of the surface of the cake.

6. Chill the cake thoroughly for several hours or overnight. Cheesecake ages well and is better on the second and third day after baking.

7. The slices are easily cut with unwaxed dental floss. Cut across the cake with the taut floss and pull through at the bottom.

2 tablespoons softened unsalted butter to grease the pan
½ cup graham cracker crumbs
1 ½ pounds (3 8-ounce packages) cream cheese at room temperature
Grated peel of 1 lemon
1 teaspoon vanilla extract
½ cup heavy cream
¾ cup plus 2 tablespoons sugar
4 large eggs at room temperature
2 tablespoons sour cream
¼ cup half-and-half cream

Preheat the oven to 375 degrees. For the water bath, place a rectangular baking pan, larger than the springform pan, in the oven. Pour about 1 ½ inches of water into this pan. Wrap the bottom and sides of an 8 x 3-inch springform pan with foil. Generously grease the inside of the pan with softened butter. Place the crumbs in the greased pan and shake the pan to coat the inside with the crumbs. Shake out any excess crumbs that don't adhere.

Add the cream cheese to the bowl of the electric mixer and beat until smooth. Scrape down the sides and bottom of the bowl and beat again if any lumps remain. Add the zest and vanilla. Gradually add the heavy cream and sugar, beating constantly. Scrape down sides and bottom once more to ensure a smooth consistency. Add the eggs, one at a time, beating after each is added. Finally, beat in the sour cream and half-and-half.

Pour the batter into the prepared pan. Gently place the pan into the water bath. Bake at 375 degrees for one hour and fifteen minutes. Then turn off the oven and leave the cake in its water bath for one hour with the oven door open several inches. Remove from the oven and cool on a wire rack. Run a knife around the sides of the pan and release the springform clip to unmold. Chill thoroughly.

Yield: 10 to 12 servings

N O T E : *This cheesecake may be served plain or with different toppings. Cherry or blueberry pie filling is an easy and delicious topping. Or whole fresh strawberries may be used with a glaze of melted strawberry jam.*

RUGELACH

The butter and cream cheese in this dough give these crescent-shaped cookies a delightful flakiness. This recipe makes small bite-sized rugelach. For larger rugelach you can divide the dough into four parts instead of six. The dough may be made up to two days ahead of time and refrigerated.

DOUGH:
1 cup butter at room temperature, cut into small pieces
8 ounces cream cheese at room temperature, cut into small pieces
2 cups flour
¼ teaspoon salt
1 egg yolk, beaten (reserve the egg white for the glaze)

FILLING:
1 cup sugar
1 cup walnuts
1 cup golden raisins
1 ½ teaspoons cinnamon

GLAZE:
1 egg white, lightly beaten
½ cup sugar mixed with ½ teaspoon cinnamon to make cinnamon sugar

Preheat oven to 350 degrees. Line 3 cookie sheets with parchment paper. If using fewer than 3 cookie sheets, change the paper in between batches.

Place flour, salt, butter and cream cheese in a large mixing bowl. Use a pastry blender to cut the butter and cream cheese into the flour until well blended. Add the egg yolk and gather the dough with a fork until it forms a ball. Lightly knead the dough to finish the blending process. Cut the dough into 6 equal parts and form each part into a round disc. Wrap each piece in lightly floured plastic wrap and chill for at least one hour.

Place sugar, walnuts, raisins and cinnamon in the bowl of a food processor fitted with a steel blade. Pulse until mixture is coarsely chopped. Set aside.

Place one piece of dough on a lightly floured board. Roll dough into a circle about ¼ inch thick. Sprinkle the filling evenly over the dough. Cut the circle into quarters and each quarter into 3 wedges for a total of twelve pie-shaped pieces. Roll each piece starting with the wide end so that the point ends up on top of the rugelach. Place rugelach on the prepared cookie sheet and bend into a crescent shape. Brush with beaten egg white and sprinkle generously with cinnamon sugar. Repeat the entire process with the other five parts of dough. Two portions of dough will yield 23-25 pieces which will fill one cookie sheet. Bake at 350 degrees for 18 minutes.

Yield: 6 dozen rugelach

N O T E S : *Using a new, clean paint brush works better for glazing small pastries than a larger pastry brush.*

A silicone baking mat also works well for lining the cookie sheet in this recipe instead of parchment paper. I just wash and dry it off in between batches.

Rugelach (left) and poppy seed ring cookies (right, page 129)

CHAPTER 9

TAMMUZ,
AV AND ELUL

TAMMUZ, AV AND ELUL

DATES *of* THE JEWISH HOLIDAYS IN TAMMUZ, AV AND ELUL

TAMMUZ:
17 MINOR FAST DAY
Commemorating the invasion of Jerusalem by the Babylonians in 586 B.C.E.

AV:

9 TISHA B'AV, MAJOR FAST DAY
Tradition has it that both Temples were destroyed on this date. In 586 B.C.E., the Babylonians destroyed the Temple and exiled our people to Babylonia. In 70 C.E., the Romans destroyed the Second Temple.

This sad period has dietary implications in that traditional Jews do not eat meat or meat products during the eight days preceding the fast (excepting Shabbat).

ELUL:
While there are no holidays in Elul, this month is punctuated by the heightened anticipation of the coming High Holidays. The shofar is sounded in the synagogue each morning, and special penitential prayers (Selichot) are added to the liturgy.

TAMMUZ, AV AND ELUL

It is convenient to think of the twelve months of the Jewish Year in quarters. The first three months of the popular year — Tishri, Cheshvan, and Kislev — represent Return. We return to our work, to our schooling, to our routines. In a more profound context, we Return in the Hebrew sense of "Tshuvah". Through self-examination, we Return to God and to the best within ourselves. The holidays in this period represent different kinds of Return — from the blast of the Shofar on Rosh Hashanah indicating personal Return, from the Sukkah indicating Return to Israel, and the Return to the Temple on Chanukah. The foods we eat during this quarter are rich and hearty, evocative of family, warmth and togetherness.

The second quarter of months —Tevet, Shevat and Adar — are the months representing Promise. Though winter may be here, Tu B'Shevat signals the promise of spring. Purim promises salvation. These two minor holidays fall right in the middle of the month when the moon is full.

The third quarter contains the months representing Peoplehood — Nisan, Iyyar and Sivan. To be a people, two things are needed — a home and a creed. On Passover, in Nisan, we attain freedom. On Shavuot, in Sivan, we attain our Law, our Torah. In the middle month, Iyyar, we celebrate Israel Independence Day. The foods are symbolic and dramatic. We evolve from the matzah, the "bread of affliction", to the "first fruits" of Shavuot. In contrast to hurriedly baked thin wafers, we now eat the barley and the grains and the fruits which we ourselves harvest and enjoy in complete freedom.

We come now to the fourth quarter of months — Tammuz, Av and Elul. These are the months of Reflection and Readiness. We contemplate the destruction of the Temple with two fast days, one obscure, one well-known. But we also contemplate the destruction of the Temple within ourselves by the sins which we have committed over the past year.

On the 17th of Tammuz, the Babylonians under Nebuchadnezzar finally invaded Jerusalem. Three weeks later, on the 9th of Av, they destroyed the First Temple, and our people were exiled to Babylonia. The period between these two days is somber, and Tisha B'Av itself a day of infinite sadness. Except on the Sabbath, meat is not eaten during the first eight days of Av. The 9th of Av, Tisha B'Av, is the only "full fast" on our calendar besides Yom Kippur. That is, we fast from the night before for more than twenty-four hours, well into the next night (all other fasts are from dawn to dusk). Finally, in Elul, we turn from national reflection to personal reflection. The Shofar is blown every day to remind us to repair the breaches within our own bodies and souls. We say *Selichot*, prayers of penitence. The cycle is completed. We are ready for a New Year.

A DAIRY DINNER MENU *for* AV

Sliced Fish

•

Heirloom Tomato Salad

•

Corn Pudding

•

Toasted Coconut Cream Pie

SLICED FISH

2 large onions, sliced
½ cup white wine
½ cup water
Salt and pepper
2 pounds of fish such as sliced halibut, flounder filets or scrod
1 cup tomato sauce or 1 pound fresh sliced tomatoes
2 tablespoons chopped parsley

In a large skillet, fry onions until golden. Add wine, water, salt and pepper. Add the fish. Pour the tomato sauce over the fish or place a slice of fresh tomato on each piece of fish. Sprinkle with parsley. Cover and simmer for ½ hour.

Yield: 8 servings

HEIRLOOM TOMATO SALAD

4 large heirloom tomatoes
3 tablespoons olive oil
1 tablespoon red wine vinegar
Salt and pepper to taste
¼ teaspoon dried oregano leaves
2 tablespoons fresh sweet basil, chopped

Slice tomatoes and arrange on a serving platter. Sprinkle with oil, vinegar, salt, pepper, oregano leaves and sweet basil leaves. Serve at room temperature.

Yield: 8 servings

CORN PUDDING

2 cups fresh corn kernels, cut off the cob
½ cup flour
4 teaspoons sugar
1 teaspoon salt
¼ cup (½ stick) unsalted butter, melted
4 large eggs
4 cups whole milk

Preheat oven to 450 degrees. Grease an 8-cup baking dish or soufflé dish.

Combine corn, flour, sugar, salt and butter in a bowl and mix to blend well. Beat the eggs with the milk in a bowl and stir into the corn mixture. Pour into a greased baking dish. Bake at 450 degrees for 40-45 minutes or until set.

Yield: 8 servings

TOASTED COCONUT CREAM PIE

This is a family recipe from my sister-in-law Barbara. The filling is airy and delicious. Therefore it is well worth the trouble of making the custard and whipping the egg whites and the cream. Using the deep-dish frozen pie shells from the market works well for this recipe (one has enough work to do making the filling). This recipe makes two pies.

This is a recipe which requires one's full attention. For example, I stand by the oven door while the coconut toasts because it can burn in an instant. Constant whisking of the milk/egg/sugar mixture will prevent curdling the eggs. And beating the whipped cream to the point of soft peaks, and no further, will prevent it from turning to butter. But making this recipe is well worth the effort. It is one of my favorite desserts.

PIE SHELLS:
Two 9-inch deep-dish frozen pie shells *(from the freezer section of the grocery)*

FILLING:
1 ½ cups sweetened, flaked coconut
1 package plain gelatin
⅓ cup cold water
1 cup whole milk
3 eggs, separated
⅔ cup sugar
1 pint heavy cream
1 teaspoon vanilla extract
Dash of salt

Preheat the oven to 375 degrees.

FOR THE PIE SHELLS:
Line each pie shell with a square of oiled foil. Place a generous handful of pastry weights or dried beans over the foil to prevent the pie shells from blistering during baking. Bake pie shells for 10 minutes or until edges of the crust are light brown. Remove from oven, remove foil and weights, and cool thoroughly on racks.

Lower the oven temperature to 325 degrees.

FOR THE TOASTED COCONUT TOPPING:
Spread ½ cup coconut in a thin layer on a cookie sheet. Bake at 325 degrees

until coconut starts to turn light brown. This process should take 4-5 minutes if the coconut is moist and fresh. If the coconut is dry, it may brown in just 3 minutes. The important point is to stand at the oven and remove the coconut as soon as it starts to brown, because it continues to brown on the hot cookie sheet after being removed from the oven. Allow to cool and transfer to a bowl.

FOR THE FILLING:

In a small bowl, sprinkle gelatin over the cold water and set aside. Place milk in the top part of a double boiler over barely simmering water until it is warm to the touch. In a bowl, whisk egg yolks and sugar together, and add gradually to the milk while continuing to whisk the milk-egg mixture. Continue to whisk until slightly thickened or until mixture coats a spoon. This process takes at least 7-8 minutes (or longer), so patience is a must. As with any custard, constant stirring over moderate heat will avoid scrambling the eggs. Initially the egg mixture will foam up to a light yellow color. As the custard nears completion, the foam subsides and the egg mixture thickens slightly and takes on a darker lemon color. At this point the custard will "coat a spoon" and it should be removed from the heat. Remove the custard from heat and let stand for a few minutes. Add gelatin mixture and stir well. Allow to cool thoroughly.

Beat the heavy cream with the vanilla until it forms soft peaks. In a separate mixing bowl, beat the egg whites with the salt until stiff. In a large bowl, fold egg whites and cream into the cooled custard. Fold in 1 cup of the coconut. Pour into the 2 pie shells. Sprinkle the toasted coconut on top of the pies. Chill pies at least 3-4 hours or overnight.

Yield: 2 pies
NOTE: *The pie shells and toasted coconut topping may be prepared the day before.*

MONTHS *of* THE JEWISH YEAR

Month Number and Name in Modern Usage	Approximate Corresponding Gregorian Month	Traditional Days of Observances		Month Number and Name in the Bible
7 TISHRI	September - October	1-2 3 10 15-22 23	ROSH HASHANAH Fast of Gedaliah YOM KIPPUR SUKKOT SIMCHAT TORAH	7 ETANEEM
8 CHESHVAN	October - November			8 BUL
9 KISLEV	November - December	25	Chanukah	
10 TEVET	December - January	10	Fast of the Tenth of Tevet	
11 SHEVAT	January - February	15	New Year for the Trees (Tu B'Shevat)	
12 ADAR	February - March	13 14 15	Fast of Esther Purim Purim in Walled Cities	
13 ADAR II *Leap Year*	March		In leap year, the above observances are celebrated in Adar II. Adar I has no holidays in a leap year.	
1 NISAN	March - April	15 27	PASSOVER Holocaust Commemoration Day (Yom Hasho'ah)	1 AVIV
2 IYYAR	April - May	5 18	Israel Independence Day Lag Ba'omer	2 ZIV
3 SIVAN	May - June	6-7	SHAVUOT	
4 TAMMUZ	June - July	17	Fast of the Seventeenth of Tammuz	
5 AV	July - August	9	Fast of Ninth of Av (Tisha B'Av)	
6 ELUL	August - September			

APPENDIX I

PEARLS AND PITFALLS FOR THE HOLIDAY COOK

When freezing foods ahead of time, I do so in a specific order. For instance, about 2 to 3 weeks before the High Holidays I make chicken soup. I do this first so that I can strain and chill the broth overnight. I will then skim off the chicken fat which I freeze separately from the broth. I then use the chicken fat when I make chopped liver and kasha varnishkes. Another example would be freezing peaches and plums available in August for fruit cobblers made in September for the holidays.

Each festival presents its own set of joys and challenges for the holiday cook. For instance, nothing imparts the joyous arrival of spring and the Passover holiday for me more than the fragrance of fresh dill which I chop with parsley and add to my chicken soup. But of course I have to remember to buy the dill in a timely fashion, so that it's there when I need it. So here are some thoughts on the challenges that seem to occur every year.

HARD-TO-FIND ITEMS

The holiday shopping list always has one or two items that are difficult to find or that disappear from the supermarket shelves quickly. When I see these, I buy them early to avoid running around to different stores at the last minute. Here's my list according to holiday.

Rosh Hashanah: The bow tie egg noodles for kasha varnishkes; medium granulation kasha; honey (you can never have enough); lemons (good for so many uses). Parsley root from the produce section may not be available in all markets. If obtainable, it does add a nice flavor to the soup.

Break the Fast: Dried fruit and candied ginger to be used for making schnecken; poppy seeds for poppy seed cake.

Sukkot: Canned pumpkin (NOT pumpkin pie filling) for pumpkin cranberry bread; pumpkin pie spice and dried cranberries for the same pumpkin cranberry bread.

Thanksgiving: Unsalted crackers for chestnut stuffing; cornbread stuffing mix; canned whole cranberries; fresh cranberries; lots of onions; carrots and celery; heavy duty foil to line the roasting pan. Make sure you have the correctly sized roasting pan and rack which fit your oven.

Chanukah: Paper towels (you need a great many for latkes); an extra five pounds of potatoes to make a second batch if needed.

Purim: The excellent Baker® brand jarred fillings for hamantaschen (poppy seed and cherry seem to disappear from the supermarket shelves the fastest); poppy seeds for baking.

Passover: Parsley root and parsnips for soup; matzah crackers for serving with chopped liver; eggs: I buy two or three dozen at a time and never seem to have enough after I get through with all of the kugels, sponge cakes and matzah brei; and, of course, fresh dill and parsley.

Shavuot: Farmer cheese for blintzes; sour cream and blueberry and cherry pie filling to top the blintzes.

TECHNIQUE:

It is important to read the recipe several times and be sure that all of the ingredients are on hand. A good habit to cultivate is the *"mise en place"*. This French term refers to the technique of measuring out all of the ingredients for a recipe before starting any cooking or baking. I like the small glass flameproof French bowls that come in many sizes to measure out the separate components of each recipe. Once the tedious chore of measuring is completed, the combining and cooking of the ingredients is so much more fun and efficient. And you won't be subjected to the unpleasant task of running out to the store at the last minute for some missing ingredient.

The temperature of ingredients is an essential consideration in baking. It is preferable to have eggs at room temperature. Egg whites mount higher when they are at room temperature, and therefore I put the eggs out on the counter on the morning of the day that I'll be baking. The recipe will specify whether the shortening should be cold or at room temperature. In general, for pie and pastry crusts the shortening needs to be chilled for a lighter and flakier crust. For cakes and cookies, the shortening should be at room temperature for easier incorporation into other ingredients and smoother texture. And finally, when working with dough and crust recipes, the recipe will specify whether the dough needs to be chilled before being rolled. The chilling process accomplishes two things. It allows the gluten in the flour to relax so the dough is not too elastic, which makes it difficult to roll. And the chilling keeps the shortening firm, which again makes the rolling out process much easier.

Unless otherwise specified, all-purpose flour is used. In the baking recipes assume that flour is sifted first and then measured. I sift the flour into a large bowl, and then spoon the sifted flour into a measuring cup. I then level off the flour with the flat side of a knife. Since baking requires more exact measuring than does cooking, good technique is essential.

The subject of pan size is important. I have tried to be specific about pan sizes for consistent and good results.

I have two mixing bowls for my standing mixer. I reserve the second bowl for beating egg whites when I make sponge cakes, since the bowl used for that purpose needs to be clean and free of any grease or oil in order for the egg whites to mount properly.

APPENDIX II

NOTES ON THE DIETARY LAWS

This book adheres to the guidelines of Kashrut, the system of Jewish laws, principles and practices relating to the preparation and consumption of food. I will touch on a few such guidelines, but the subject is vast, and further sources should be consulted for a full understanding of these principles.

1. Meat and dairy are considered two families of food products and may never be consumed together. A waiting period is therefore prescribed before consuming dairy products after meat products, and vice versa. Separate dishes and utensils are used for meat and milk. A Rabbi should be consulted for more specifics.

2. Animals, birds and sea creatures are considered kosher if they meet certain biblical and Talmudic criteria. For example, an animal must chew the cud and possess a split hoof. Thus, the cow is considered kosher, but the pig — which does not chew the cud — is not. As another example, salmon is fine to eat, but shellfish are not. Chicken is kosher, but birds of prey are not.

3. Even kosher animals must be ritually slaughtered, and only certain parts of the animal may be consumed. The blood must be completely drained from the animal. If a blood spot is noted when cracking an egg, that egg should be discarded.

4. There is a third family of foods which may be eaten with dairy or with meat. This group of foods is called "parve", and includes fruits and vegetables, eggs, acceptable fish, and many other foods. So, for example, tuna may be served as an appetizer before a meat meal, or enjoyed with a glass of milk. Milk and meat together, however — not kosher!

5. In this volume, all-vegetable shortening is specified for recipes listed in menus that contain meat or chicken. Most margarines in stores contain milk products such as milk solids. Parve margarine can be found in the kosher section of the supermarket. The label should be checked for the exact ingredients. Of course, if the recipe is not being used in a meat meal, then butter may be substituted.

6. Kosher gelatin made from vegetable products is available in the kosher section of the supermarket or in certain markets which carry products geared for vegetarians or vegans. Be sure to read the label for directions since these products may jell more quickly than conventional gelatin. In addition, when adding crushed pineapple to the recipe, drain off juice and simmer pineapple for one minute to destroy an enzyme which may interfere with the jelling process.

7. With respect to kashrut, some observant Jews do not mix meat and fish together in the same dish. Since Worcestershire sauce contains anchovies, Orthodox tradition prescribes that, if used with meat, the sauce must contain no more than a certain percentage of anchovies in the sauce. A Rabbi should be consulted for further guidance.

8. During Passover, all leavening products such as yeast, baking powder and baking soda are forbidden. In addition, grains such as corn and rice are prohibited in the Ashkenazic tradition. Variations in the Sephardic tradition are not addressed in this volume.

9. Ⓚ or Ⓤ and other symbols on a product package designate a food as kosher (though not necessarily for Passover — that's a whole world of kashrut beyond the scope of this book).

The books of Exodus, Leviticus and Deuteronomy articulate the injunctions which form the basis of the dietary laws. These ordinances were later expanded in the Talmud (2nd-5th century CE) and the Shulchan Arukh (late 16th century). Discussion and dialogue about kashrut continue to the present day. It is a system that has united the Jewish people for millenia, and has provided the world with a rich, traditional cuisine.

CONTRIBUTORS

I am grateful to all of the following friends and family who generously shared their wonderful recipes. Every recipe is special to me. Recipes are derivative, and the origin of a recipe may become blurred over a period of time. My apologies for any inaccuracies in this list. For a recipe with no attribution, either the source is lost in time or I have created it myself.

Emma Benjamin ....Tu B'Shevat Treats
Betty Carney... Honey Cake
Rick Carocci .... Rick's Noodle Kugel
Thelma Chase .... Eggplant Bake
Tuna Salad with Walnuts and Cocktail Onions
Coconut Pound Cake
Susan Callen ....Gazpacho
Rita Day and Patti Goldstein..Carrot Ring
Jack Ecklund and Derrick Niederman ....Crêpes for Blintzes
with a French Flair
Fannie Fertig ....Never-Fail Kneidlach
Cucumber Salad
Mimi Gormezano .... Endive, Grapefruit and Avocado Salad
Bobbie Halpern...Bobbie's Passover Sponge Cake
Betsy Klausman...Quick Apple Cake
Marjorie Lesser ....Coq Au Vin
Chocolate Mousse
Helen Levy ....Chanukah Sugar Cookies
Dr. Helen Metzger and Dr. Sol Kleiner ....Matzah Balls (Kneidlach)
Kasha Varnishkes
Ilse Meyer... Noodle and Rice Kugel
Gloria Osland ....Gloria's Heimish Fruit Compote
Elisabeth Proske .... Easy Lemon Pie
Annamarie Pyfer..Barbecued Brisket
Jewish Apple Cake
RSVP International, *Maker of the Endurance® fish poacher*
....Cold Poached Salmon
Shirley Robinson ....Oatmeal Lace Cookies
Pumpkin Cranberry Bread

GENERAL INDEX

(An Index by Food Category Follows)

INDEX BY FOOD CATEGORY

NOTES